How I Lost A Million Dollars Twice

And Other "Brilliant" Adventures

Published by Taylor Young at Smashwords
Copyright 2013 by Taylor Young
Cover by Vila Design

Introduction

Yep, at a relatively young age, I lost the opportunity to pocket a million dollars, not once, but twice. Fuck! Not to worry, though. Some painfully great life changing lessons were learned through it all. At times, getting kicked in the nards is just the wake-up call needed to wise up.

Don't assume this is some boring stiff's focused guide to personal finances. It isn't at all. While there are plenty of rants about the do's and don'ts with your money, which I learned by stubbornly screwing up repeatedly, this is an adventure of eclectic stories in my occasionally out of control life. The connection between all these tirades is that they relate to money somehow, and me losing a bunch of it because I had my head up my ass.

From blown vehicles, horrible houses, mountains of debt, greasy food, yappy dogs and pink pigs, to money scams, rock star music, inheritances gone AWOL, and tiny bathrooms, please come with me on some train wrecks. Learn from my mistakes, squandering my chances of being a multi-millionaire.

Maybe some of these things can save your butt from a good kicking, too.

Chapter 1

Twice In A Day

As I pulled off an exit from Interstate 90 at Ritzville, Washington, to head south on Highway 395 to Richland, I was surprised to see a Highway Patrol car sitting on the right side of the road at the exit. "What the fuck?" I immediately thought. It looked almost as if it was waiting for me. After I passed it, the patrol car took off behind me. I wasn't overly surprised. "Hmm, I wasn't speeding," I said to myself.

After a moment, from my rear view mirror, I could see the dreaded flashing lights suddenly appear. The cruiser quickly caught up with me and stayed right behind me, obviously my cue to pull over. I signaled and pulled over to the right side of the road. My 1969 money green Cadillac Coupe DeVille, with its 472 cubic inch 375 horsepower engine, rumbled to a stop.

The patrolman got out of his car and walked toward me. From my outside mirror, I could see him looking at the back of the car. Maybe that fake metal stick-on plastic fish would be to my benefit about now. As he got closer I could see him looking into the back seat. I wasn't worried, because there was nothing there anymore.

I zoomed down my electric window. "Afternoon, officer," I said as he approached my side of the car.

"Can I see your driver's license and registration?" he asked.

As I handed the documents to him, he asked, "Where are you going?"

"Richland," I said. "That's where I live."

"Where have you been today?" he asked.

"I was visiting family in Montana. Butte. Been driving back from there all day."

He continued, "We got reports of someone in a green car speeding and throwing out beer cans at trucks."

I was stunned. "Wow," I said.

"Was that you?" he asked. "Have you been drinking?"

"No, I haven't," I lied, looking right at him. "That wasn't me."

He looked inside the car through the windows again and returned back to his patrol car.

"Oh, shit," I said out loud as I waited, watching him in his patrol car from my rear view mirror. If he did a breath test on me, I probably wouldn't pass it, though I doubt I looked drunk at all. And I wasn't really. I'd just been slowly sipping on beers all day long. And yes, a few empty cans may have slipped out the window. If a truck happened to be in the way of a few of them, why was that my problem?

After what seemed like a long time, I watched him get back out of his car and walk towards my Coupe DeVille.

"I am *screwed*," I thought.

"Okay, drive safe," he said, handing my license and registration back to me.

"Thanks, officer," I said, not believing what just took place.

My heart was really pounding. I eased the Caddy back onto the road. "Holy crap!" I yelled out loud. "Woohoo!" I couldn't believe my luck. I drove like a grandma all the way home.

He must have called ahead, because after I got to Richland and as I rolled through West Richland, almost home, a town cop pulled me over on the main drag, towards the far end of town.

"What the hell, now?" I thought.

He walked up to my rolled down window. "Going a little fast?" he said.

Now, I was *not* speeding, I'm sure. But having learned a lesson years earlier about arguing with a cop over running a red light on my way to Mission Ridge ski area, whereby I had adamantly insisted the light hadn't turned red yet, I knew it was best not to argue. That ticket had cost me time off of work to drive two hours to pay the fine anyway.

"Sorry about that," I said, "I guess I wasn't paying attention to my speed."

After asking for the usual documents, he asked, "You been drinking?"

"No," I half lied, since it had been several hours.

"How come your eyes are so bloodshot?" he asked.

"I just drove five hundred miles from Montana today," I said, looking straight at him. "I'm so tired."

"Hmm," he said, studying my license and registration. "Okay, just watch your speed through town."

"Thanks," I said, again, not believing my good fortune. Was it the silvery fish stuck on the trunk of the car or what? I did another "Woohoo!" and headed immediately for home.

Before you think, "what a drunk" or "what a hypocrite," at least consider that I'd recently gotten divorced. Drinking was just one of my more pleasurable ways of dealing with my stress. It was just a harmless phase. No harm, no foul. Right!

In disbelief of how the day had gone, I pondered everything as I drove home. At least I had a lovely home sweet home to go to, my refuge in the wilderness. Or so that was how the dream was supposed to go.

In reality, it was a refinanced mobile home on acreage purchased with a credit card. Yep, I was up to my eyeballs in plenty of other trouble, of which, drinking was the least of it.

$$$$$$$$

Chapter 2

Twelve Acres

"Of course I have the money," I lied through my teeth to my elderly neighbor. Technically, I did have the money, though.

"As you sure?" she asked. "I don't want to set up the title transfer unless you really have the cash."

Just a few weeks before this conversation this same elderly woman, who lived down the hill in a cute little house in the trees by the river, had driven up to my place in the sun baked sagebrush. Turns out, her husband had died a few years before and she was interested in selling a piece of land, twelve acres, that adjoined my existing property. She wanted to know if I might be interested in buying it.

My existing property was my dream land. Nine and one half acres of sagebrush out in the middle of nowhere, on a hill with a view of the Yakama River. Not just a view of the river, but a panoramic half mile view of it. And facing the west too, so the best sunsets.

There was nothing like it. It was a damn oddity really, consisting of three quarters of a mile of old railroad right of way. But I loved it. Think about it; a hundred foot wide swath of land by three quarters of a mile long, curving through sage brush, a rock "canyon" and finally ending on a secluded hillside overlooking the river. I lived at the very end.

I had financed the railroad land through the seller and then used my credit cards to put in a well and septic system. All was looking grand. Then I did a dumb ass thing. Like taking a whore to a wedding, I relocated the mobile home that I'd been stuck with after the divorce, from the trailer park out to my dream land, instead of just building a house.

If only I knew then that I'd take more of a financial beating later, I'd have sold that mobile home at the trailer park and gladly taken whatever loss I had to just to get out of it. I should have held out to build a house from scratch on this land. What was I thinking! But that's what happens when numb nut thinking collides with impatience and a bunch of empty credit cards.

But in the end I "got 'er done" and had my mobile home moved and set up right at the very end of my stretch of heaven. One of my neighbors, who stumbled up the hill to my place through the sagebrush with a glass of wine in his hand one evening to complain about the loud music booming through their tranquil neighborhood, said he was nonetheless amazed at how fast I was able to buy the land, put in a well, put in a septic systems, get all the permits, move my mobile home, and get moved in. Just how in the *hell* did he not spill that wine?

So I was gloating a bit. I took that as a big pat on the back for having been a great general contractor on my first attempt at it ever. Encouraged, I moved forward with my plans.

I refinanced the place and rolled the mobile home debt, land debt, credit card charges for the well and septic system, and credit card charges for the home move and set up all into one nice neat mortgage. I should have stopped there. But stupidity usually has an uglier and even dumber twin brother.

And I would have stopped there, had it not been for that old lady from down the hill. She tempted me with an irresistible offer of a prime twelve acre plot right above the very end of my three quarters of a mile swath. It was bordered by a pretty large vineyard region. This extra land would allow bigger dreams to come true: Pastures, corals, horses, riding arena, an oasis at the end of my very long secluded driveway.

So I did what any savvy land shark would do. I got a thirty thousand dollar cash advance on one of my credit cards and "paid cash" for the twelve acres. That was my little white lie to the old lady down the hill. The deal went through without a hitch.

And I didn't stop there. I rented, with other credit cards, bulldozers, backhoes and other equipment to level a huge horse riding area, level other areas, scrape, smooth, dig, and eventually move bundles of fence posts delivered from Idaho (paid for by, you guessed it, credit cards).

It was so fun being the general contractor and heavy equipment operator on my little piece of paradise. I buried a frickin' truck chassis in my yard for crying out loud! What a blast. I buried many a beer can too.

All said and done, I racked up a total of sixty-five thousand dollars on credit cards (thirty thousand of it was from the land bought from the old lady). And the place was taking shape. So was I. I worked my ass off. I never worked so hard, physically. And long. Nearly every spare minute after my normal full-time job was spent working at the place putting up fences and corrals, doing various rock-work, and watering and mowing.

One thing was lacking, however. Greenery. I did have a lawn but I had to water it manually with above ground hoses. I never got around to planting trees and putting in a real watering system because I ran out of credit first. Oh, how I wished I'd put in water lines and planted trees and a decent lawn first! It would have made resale so much easier. But, as I said, the uglier twin brother had already arrived.

The mistake I made in not seeking advice about this grandiose plan of mine was that I wrongly assumed I could refinance after the "improvements" were completed and then pay off all my credit card debt. What I failed to realize, like a gopher standing straight up on the side of the highway staring at the tire veering towards it, was that merely having all that credit card debt made me ineligible for a new mortgage. I had too high of a debt to income level and just plain too much consumer debt.

"But the whole reason I want the mortgage is to *pay off* the very debts that you say make me ineligible," I would argue. Why couldn't they get this through their thick fucking skulls!

It was no use. The banks would not help me. Mortgage brokers could get me nothing. I basically was stuck with my original mortgage for the mobile home and nine and one half acres, and on top of it the sixty five thousand dollars' worth of improvements put on my credit cards.

The sad thing was that many of the credit card companies had allowed me to transfer balances for zero interest for a limited time. And so I bounced some money back and forth for a while to hold off the wolves. But the time was up. My interest rates shot up, and so did my payments. I tried opening some more credit cards, but was denied repeatedly. What a sham. I was pretty humiliated at this point.

So I did what anyone in my situation would do. I treated myself to a little reward for all my hard work. My last big expenditure was a big screen TV, seventeen hundred dollars, put on the last available limit on my last available credit card.

All my credit lines were tapped out and used up. Quickly, I found myself barely able to make my monthly payments, even though I was an engineer with ten years of experience and pay to match. Some months I went to one of those rip off payday loan establishments for a few hundred dollar advance. Seems like the equivalent annual interest rate was about two hundred percent. Talk about humiliating to go in there and tell them what you make and ask for a two week advance for two hundred bucks.

Some people handle divorce or other stress by overeating and putting on weight. Me? I just spent every dollar I earned and could borrow. And sometimes for fun I took that old Cadillac Coupe DeVille on a mad adventure. Beer cans, schmeer cans!

$$$$$$$

Chapter 3

Planes, Trains and Automobiles

Like a whore house on a Saturday night, I was visited by Murphy many a time after I reached the end of my financial rope. Usually he was carrying a monkey wrench or a cup of sugar to dump in my gas tank.

My beloved Coupe DeVille was the first to bite the dust. Whether it was my excessive pedal to the floor driving style or Marvin's Mystery Oil going AWOL or Murphy himself slipping some magic dust into the gas, a serious clacking noise started in the engine and, although I babied it after that, she eventually froze up. My "expert" diagnosis determined that the engine needed major work, something I could not afford to do, nor wanted to do.

The old girl was parked and abandoned out by the pump house on my dream land. Wasps built a monster nest in the engine compartment, so I stayed clear from then on.

The Caddy was sold for scrap, pretty much given away in a deal I made over the phone from work. After putting a For Sale ad in the paper listing a ridiculous price, some moron called me and actually wanted the old bug infested heap. I never met the guy at all. Leaving the title, registration, and keys in the car one day before I went to work, the buyer came out with a flatbed trailer and picked up the car. He hid the money in my pump house as we agreed. It's one of the few deals that I didn't get burned on, other than the fact that he got a steal on a flawless vintage car body with perfect glass and interior. Oh boy.

With the Caddy gone bust, like the most popular plastic surgery for blond, B-size Hollywood actresses, it was a little tougher getting around. Luckily I had a backup rig. I had bought an old primer gray Chevy 4X4 pickup truck with a credit card cash advance a year earlier when I still had credit. It had become my "ranch truck." It was a little impressive too, with its lifted suspension, chrome wheels, knobby tires, and beautiful sounding rumbling exhaust. The body was perfect too. But it was rough riding as hell, noisy as a nagging ex-wife, and the worst gas hog you could possibly have. It was a hassle for hauling around my guitars and amps because you couldn't hide them away like I could in the three-corpse Caddy trunk.

So I put an ad in the paper to sell or trade the truck and ended up trading it for an even older Toyota pickup. That little Toyota was like gold to me. Finally, some peace and quiet, decent gas mileage, and a CD player too. It was all white, with a white topper. I could haul stuff around in the back, and keep it under cover and locked up.

All was peachy for a while. But soon the Toyota bit the dust too, even though I babied that rig. I'd been partying one evening and was heading home. On the county road leading out to my dream land, it simply lost power and died on the side of the road. And what was the first rig to come up the road? A frickin' cop car!

"What the hell!" I said once I recognized what it was. I played real dumb and quickly asked the off duty officer for a ride home. And once again, I dodged a bullet by him not smelling alcohol on my breath. He gladly gave me a ride all the way out to my house. I was relieved to ride in the back seat, though it seemed like a bad omen.

Again, my "expert" diagnosis determined that the engine needed major work, something I could not afford to do nor wanted to do.

Without a vehicle and without any money or available credit card funds, I did what any sane person would do. I walked into a Dodge dealer one evening and drove away a brand spanking new Dodge Neon with no money down. I didn't even test drive it. I just walked out onto the lot, pointed to the cheapest, smallest new car, and said, "That's the one. I'll take it." After the paperwork was signed and as the keys were handed to me, they all clapped for me, for God's sake. It was one of those marketing gimmicks to help you not have buyer's remorse later, I guess. I was stoked.

The next day, the dealer's finance department called me, saying my credit did not go through and to please return the car. Highly embarrassed, I drove the car back to the dealer. By the time I got there, they had found a way for me to keep the car: A sixteen and a half annual percentage rate loan. I desperately signed up for it like a sailor signing up for gonorrhea treatment in the ship's medical clinic after a weekend shore leave.

Yep, that was me, a glutton for punishment.

But, oh, did I have some fun with that car. I "buried the needle" many times. One hundred and twenty miles an hour, plus! Surprised the heck out of me. There was this stretch of paved county road out in the vineyards, near my dream land, that was perfectly straight for a few miles. Half of it was sloped up a gentle hill so you could clearly see the whole stretch no matter which direction you were speeding. There were only vineyards on the sides of the road all the way up and down. So I'd get my Neon going fast enough along that stretch to bury the needle, going both directions. What a blast!

Often, I'd stop by that road on the way home just for fun.

What I soon learned is that the front wheel bearings were not intended for that kind of speed because they started making noise within the first year. And I was making a lot of noise too. Broke and alone, I hung out mostly at my place overlooking the river, waiting for something to give.

Sure, the warranty paid to fix the wheel bearings. But it's probably a good thing I couldn't see into the future because I would have been more than depressed knowing that within two years of buying that car, it would cost me five thousand bucks to get out of that rip off loan because I was so upside down.

This was a new low in my life. Broke, no savings, no credit, a loser car deal, slave to my job, and not seeing a way out had me constantly worried and stressed. So I drank and smoked cigarettes all the more.

During that period, more than occasionally, I even smoked marijuana, something I hadn't done since I was a teenager. Every once in a while, I'd feel guilty about the pot smoking, though, and I'd shake out the bag on my land in the wind. Shit, if I would have just had my water system in place maybe I would have soon discovered some valuable plants. Probably a good thing my land was as dry as a bone, a perfect picture of my life.

That was about the time I met her.

$$\$\$\$\$\$\$\$$$

Chapter 4

Her & My Money

From our very first date, I liked her a lot. After several dates, I couldn't get enough of her company. She had that "X" factor. You just know when you meet someone like that and it just clicks. I had a hunch this could be for the long haul.

Yet we were radically different. The rebel was me, and she was the preacher's daughter who really had been a good kid and still was. She liked sappy love songs and I liked hard rock. She didn't drink a drop of alcohol and I was quite good at it. She said she wasn't going to marry a smoker and I had been smoking cigarettes for decades and pot lately too, though I quit both as soon as she told me that.

We talked about everything except one scary topic: money and my lack thereof. The only thing I told her was that I was scared about layoffs at work. A layoff would have forced me into bankruptcy (I didn't tell her that, though). And little did she know that some of our nice meals that I put on my credit card on our date nights would be paid back by us later with interest.

Yet, after the wedding date was set, we still had discussed everything but money. Our pre-marriage counselor urged us to tackle this topic. So I fessed up. My fiancé was floored when she learned how much debt I had. And she saw firsthand how upset and angry the whole thing made me. I asked her what she thought about the possibility of me going bankrupt.

She didn't answer that question. And instead of running, she bought me an audio book on personal finances that I could listen to in the car. I still remember exactly where I was driving, listening to the author's narration, when the light bulb went on big time and it finally hit me just how out of control I was in every way with money. All of a sudden I had this strong burning resolve to right things. All of a sudden I had a desire to get smart with money.

So we read more and studied and talked and planned and talked some more about money and how we were going dig us out of the hole I was bringing into our marriage. And it was during those learning sessions that I first realized, no, calculated, that I had already given up a million dollars in my life.

$$$$$$$

Chapter 5

My First Million

I'd been working since I was fourteen years old. By any conservative estimate of stock market returns since that time, saving a mere two hundred dollars a month could have easily grown to well over a million dollars by the time, well, not yet. But damn, I could have at least looked forward to retiring early. I re-did the math just to be sure. Yep, it was correct. The real fact, though, was that I'd squandered my first million by the time I hit my late-thirties, because I'd had the means to save much more than two hundred dollars a month since I was fourteen. Instead, decades later my net worth was negative.

It was a depressing surprise to realize just how easily time and interest rates could turn modest monthly savings into wealth. *Anyone* could to this. Anyone could *choose* to be wealthy it seemed.

Why didn't I get this simple fact when I was younger? Even an idiot could understand these concepts, so why did I not plan or even seem to care? I felt humiliated and pissed off at myself for being such a douche. I'd already thrown away a million on partying and bowing to porcelain gods, lots of cars long since recycled into Japanese tsunami walls, choking down bad pizzas, 101 channels of shit satellite TV, stupid toys and expensive musical equipment long since either in the dump or the thrift stores, and regular grazing at Denny's and McDonald's and the frozen dinner section at Safeway.

So even before we were marred, my fiancé and I planned to turn things around. We got radical. I literally sold everything I owned to get out of payments and turn stuff to cash. Many things I sold at a loss because I was upside down. One of them was that Dodge Neon. I took a five grand kick in the nards for that one. It was a painfully good lesson to learn. She bought me an old Toyota Celica with cash, a few months before we got married. I loved that car and put a lot of miles on it over the years that followed.

After the wedding, we moved to a basement apartment. We didn't buy anything extra. I worked as much overtime as I could. We slowly, one by one, paid off my credit cards: sixty-five thousand greenbacks! Then we tackled my teenaged student loans. We paid off my divorce obligations. And then we sold the hard-sell mobile home on acreage that no one could get a loan for, the last kick in the balls.

We eventually reached the end of the rainbow, after a few very tough years. We got *out of debt*. Can you believe that? No debt! My high anxiety level had just melted away. It was only then that I began to believe that we could truly become millionaires with time and compounding interest, because I could sense how much saving was possible without debt.

But I was to unexpectedly lose my chances at another million before the next decade was over.

$$$$$$$

Chapter 6

Don't Count On Anything

Do you have a rich relative? Maybe a rich uncle? I did.

In my early twenties, while working as a ranch hand in Montana, I was impressed with this uncle's financial position. He'd been a mechanical engineer all his career. He retired in his mid-fifties. He never married and never had children. He wasn't much of a traveler and lived very modestly.

He stayed living at home to take care of his aging parents and eventually inherited their home and several farms, some of which had producing oil wells on them. We all thought he just had to be loaded.

The combination of me working on the Montana ranch, which was owned by a mechanical engineer, and my uncle the mechanical engineer, inspired me to go to college to become a mechanical engineer. And not long after finishing college and moving to Washington State to work, I received a series of letters from this uncle.

Basically he was getting all his affairs in order. I thought it was a little odd that he was doing this because at that time he was only in his seventies. He said when he died he was leaving everything to me and my three brothers. House, farms, old wells, and all his investments. Of course, we never knew exactly how rich he really was. But we speculated he must have millions.

Many of his investments were in real estate, oil, and gold. One of my brothers seems to remember a conversation in which he was told the uncle had about three hundred, one ounce gold coins. Do the math. Just some of his pocket change, I guessed. He probably kept it in a hole in his basement, not trusting banks.

Over the years I forgot about the details contained in those letters. I always figured I'd someday be inheriting some money, but I truly did forget him saying he was leaving it all to us.

Nearly two decades later, my uncle died. It was sad to find out about his quick decline and passing. There was a lot of reflection and wondering why we didn't see him more over the years. It was only through the frequent letters back and forth that we ever knew him.

Curious about his Will and knowing how easy it is to get public records, many through the Internet, we soon had a copy of it. And we were surprised to find out he had changed his Will about four years prior to his death. The real shocker was that we were not in his Will anymore.

Everything went to his sister, who also never married, worked and saved her whole life, inherited some of her parents' fortune, didn't travel, lived simply and was likely loaded herself. She lived in the house just next door to my uncle. They did their financial planning together. They were both so frugal that they shared a car for crying out loud.

Apparently he and his sister had chosen just four years prior to split the potential majority of their estates among various school, library, fire department, and hospital organizations. These are good causes, so none of us nephews were upset by that. And I had bet that his sister's Will was very similar to his, as they always seemed to collaborate on such dealings.

Then I remembered those old letters and seemed to remember him telling us he was at least leaving us *something*. And that didn't seem to jive with this last Will. I had to dig through some boxes to find those old letters my uncle had sent to me. Sure enough, I had saved them.

It was a surprise to see just what he had written years earlier. In one such letter my uncle had written, "We had new wills drawn up and after two small bequests the remainder will be divided equally among you and your brothers." This same letter and subsequent letters also described the farms and oil wells to be left to us.

Our uncle wrote to us extensively and in detail about our inheritance. In another such letter to me with details about the farms he wrote, "Please put these papers with the other information I sent you regarding your inheritance." This remained unchanged through the many years since, as he was meticulous in his written communications with us.

Even when the farms were finally sold ten years prior to his death, he wrote to tell us why that happened and, true to his attention-to-detail character, communicated no further changes regarding our inheritance.

So quite frankly, I was stunned at how different his wishes seemed to be at the end. The contrast seemed a bit irrational, but definitely out of character from my uncle's previous thorough nature in communicating details with us. And although I might wonder about the soundness of my uncle and his sister's minds during the establishment of their final Wills, because of this apparent change in his demeanor, there was probably no point to debating that now, since it was all over done with.

But we were able to find out that my uncle's lawyer was currently or at one time on the Board of Directors for one of the organizations that my uncle's Will specifically named as leaving money to.

No matter, in the end here is the second million dollars I lost. Even if it wasn't a million that I would have inherited, if at least I could have invested whatever the inheritance was at the time it would surely have grown to well over a million or millions by the time I retired. Bummer.

Moral of this story: Don't count on a penny from anyone else.

$$$$$$$

Chapter 7

Find A Scapegoat

After my uncle's death, I found myself pretty pissed off by the stark realization that, at a relatively young age, I'd lost two opportunities to be a millionaire, one was flat out squandered away and the other, a long standing promise that vanished.

On a side note, sorry if you feel betrayed by the title of this book. Did you actually think I'd made a million dollars and lost it, made it back, and lost it a second time? If that were really the case then I might merely be part of a statistic in someone else's book titled, *Why More Millionaires Jump To Their Deaths Than Any Other Demographic*, or perhaps some other best seller, *Why More Millionaires Jump From Buildings Than Bridges*.

Which do you think hurts more: To have had a million and lost it or to know you could have had a million but squandered it before you ever had it?

I can only tell you that the one I experienced hurts too. And if you understand anything about guys, you'll know that when we hurt, we usually try to punch someone else back to make us feel better. So I decided to lash out at something or someone. It was time to blame some organization for my not being a millionaire yet. So I started looking around. It was easy to find scapegoats everywhere.

You ever have a song you strongly dislike suddenly pop into your head? And it seems to come when you're in the worst of moods already? If I was God I'd enjoy playing that game a lot on people too.

The first scapegoat popped into my mind like a bad song. I remembered the humiliation of going into that payday loan store to beg for some money. What was the name of it? Money Branch? Lending Frenzy? I don't know why, I found myself also burning with anger remembering those stupid payday store ads on TV and their pathetic caterpillar. Oh, if only I could just squash the yellow goo out of that little sneering, smiling bug. It seemed only natural to find some online thread about this company and post another scathing comment:

"Fuck You Money Branch,
You are a modern day loan shark. The credit card companies' high interest rates are a great deal compared to your rip off "services." You assholes are not doing anyone a favor with your 200% annual interest rates. What a fucking SCAM. You guys need to be run out of town, tarred and feathered, brought back to town and paraded through the streets under the bumper of a primer gray Chevy 4X4, and then made to pay back all of the money you've swindled from unsuspecting, lower income people who absolutely can't afford to keep getting reamed by your greedy tactics. You aren't doing anyone a service but yourselves, so get a clue, you morons.
---A dissatisfied customer with a grudge, a hunting rifle, an old Ford van with painted over windows, and a few thug friends who have nothing better to do than to take a dare for a few six packs of beer."

Ahh…that felt better. But it still didn't change my situation. I was still in the same fucking, disappointing boat. I'd missed a fortune twice. And even though my wife and I were trying to save like crazy now, we had started late, and it was slow going. And there were plenty of people and companies waiting in the wings to take it from us along the way if we weren't careful.

Previously, I'd had plenty of other frustrating experiences with banks, mortgage companies, and credit card companies. They were already big assholes in my mind just like the Money Branch (or whatever the hell it's called).

It seemed logical that there was a lot of blame to go around. So, by no mistake, the food industry caught my attention as being worthy of some disgust. Were they really providing a useful service to us or just costing us more money like the frickin' financial institutions?

$$\$\$\$\$\$\$\$$

Chapter 8

Love My Raisin Bran

When my wife and I first started a plan for getting out of debt, I found myself questioning the motives of everyone who sold me shit in a pretty package. Many food companies were right there. Just what was their angle for making money? Was it with me in mind, or primarily their company profits? I think we all know the answer to that.

And so one morning I opened a box of my beloved Raisin Bran, one of my favorite cereals since, well, my whole life! The first bowl was nothing but flakes. "Hmm," I thought. Obviously, it was settled quite a bit from shipping, but I wasn't too worried. I got looking at the side of the box and it said "Product of Mexico."

Now I've got nothing against the cereal manufacturer or Mexico. But why does this company think they have to make some of their highly processed food in another country to ship back to the U.S.? Surely it's because it's cheaper to make in Mexico. But do you think that box of cereal cost less to me? No damn way.

My wife sent the company an email asking why they are doing this, and of course here is their canned mumbo jumbo reply:

"Thank you for contacting us regarding the location of our manufacturing facilities. We appreciate the opportunity to respond.

[Blankity blank] is a global company with manufacturing and sales locations worldwide. Our founder, [Blankity blank], had a strong commitment to

nutrition, health and quality, which continues to drive improvement in our products and processes today. Around the world, [Blankity blank] manufacturing facilities and products follow the same [Blankity blank] quality standards, often exceeding government quality standards.

Because [Blankity blank] operates globally, our decisions take into consideration not only the conditions in the United States, but also the situation worldwide. You might imagine that the recent economic situation is of great concern to us as we assess the pricing and availability of ingredients, packaging, labor and energy. We have historically used our global network of locations to best serve our consumers in quality and cost. Likewise, we will continue to explore ways to ensure we are operating efficiently and effectively to support our business goals of overall growth and ensuring manufacturing capacity to meet current and future consumer demand.

Again, thank you for your comments. We are grateful to be able to share this perspective."

Talk about politically correct! I was actually impressed with their great word-smithing skills. But the simple translation is: "We will do nearly anything to increase profits and overall growth." We already knew that, you dip shits!

So where do they talk about the savings passed on to the customers from all this efficiency? Not there, thought so. Their brand is no cheaper than the other brands. And did you get that, "<u>often</u> exceeding government quality standards?" What's with that? Who's government? Oh, well.

Now, again, don't misunderstand. I have nothing against this company, Mexico, or Raisin Bran cereal. Love them all. But this just got me wondering even more whether certain foods and food companies are somehow causing me to lose money. I guess I shouldn't have been surprised at what I found.

$$$$$$$

Chapter 9

Oil and Water (You and Your Food)

At times we seem to be more loyal to things that harm us than the things that are really good for us. Need I make a drunken sailor and brothel comment again? But I'm talking about food here.

Take greasy foods. What is it about greasy food that we can't seem to get enough of? While driving past a fast food restaurant recently, the familiar and compelling smell of french fries suddenly filled the car. And it smelled *so* good! I love them. But I also thought about how often after stuffing my pie hole with a supersized order of those hot, greasy potato strips, the sensation turns to an unsettling clump in my gut, slight nausea, and a vow to stay away the next time.

Why do we keep doing this? We crave the fatty, salty goodness of fries and other deep fried goodies, but after eating them feel like we've just stepped onto another planet with a much higher gravitational pull. Yet we keep returning for more, like a dog to a steaming, fly-infested pile of cow dung.

In fact, while writing these paragraphs, I remembered something in the kitchen cupboard, took a break, and stuffed my face with some greasy potato chips. I know they're not good for me, but I can't help it. They're so dang tasty. Cow dung good.

The second culprit has got to be sugar, or perhaps worse, products made with high fructose corn syrup (a very processed sweetener). I'm not a doctor, but I do know this: This stuff makes you fat. And it's addicting, just like the greasy goodness foods. When I was a kid I used to just love and crave sugary candy. We just love eating and drinking things that give us pleasure.

Maybe some our most favorite "foods" are really just unhealthy addictions purposefully concocted to be irresistible by companies with a greedy agenda. And if not taken in moderation, maybe these goodies are slowly killing us, not to mention messing with our wallets.

It seems our lives are at odds with many things, just like oil and water. Do you still not believe that our food and our money are tied together? They're at odds right now. I'm telling you, there is a giant scam going on in our food supply. It's mostly done with some big wig ass wipe's profit in mind, not your health. And that may just cost you and me another million later on.

$$$$$$$

Chapter 10

Bottom Feeders

Just how significantly is the food we eat tied to our money? They're inseparable. Poor food choices relate directly to higher out-of-pocket health costs. But less money relates to poor food choices. This is the vicious cycle that I'm afraid the "bottom feeders" are stuck in. And I don't mean the fat-asses, though it could apply thanks to the food choices we're being offered.

Those who refuse to get smart with personal finances typically end up living paycheck to paycheck, or worse. If people were merely spending all they make, that would just cause one set of problems. The bigger issue is however, that many people also tap into their credit lines to increase their standard of living beyond what they earn. So they're spending all they bring in, and then some, kind of like our government does.

Being strapped for cash means more often than not the food budget will take a hit. It's funny how that works. People will go cheap on food before they'll ever think of getting rid of their cell phone or cable TV or internet or big dumb rig. People will eat and drink crap all day long before they'll drive an older, paid-for car. As a result, they are relegated to a life style of poor nutrition. But they don't see the problem.

Instead of fresh, whole vegetables, fruits, nuts and seeds, much less the organic variety which can cost more, people would much rather have lattes and their cell phone. Then they cheap out at the grocery store. Or maybe it's just simply that fatty, sugary, and salty goodness meets most people's taste bud cravings.

And surprise, most of the time these foods are cheaper because the industry has mastered the art of making food products from cheap ingredients like white flour, oils and fats, high fructose corn syrup, and sugar. Most people eat such garbage on a daily basis, even perhaps get the majority of their calorie intake from it. And as would be expected, people are generally fat, diseased, and tired.

Sadly, this is not just a problem of the poor. Many people who can afford to eat healthier food still don't, preferring the fat, salt, and sugar additions. And most people also love a diet rich in growth-enhanced and antibiotic-laced meats, puss infected pasteurized dead milk and other dairy products, abnormally produced "cage" eggs, all cooked up with genetically modified oil products. Ironically, these are the very foods that the USDA pushes on school children.

Then the "health" system picks up on our slack, providing pills for every symptom. Nutrition is seldom seen as the enemy. Instead, poor genes are seen as the cause. People are mere victims. Therefore, there is no cure or accountability, only a treatment of the symptoms. The drug companies and medical "professions" profit like crazy. And people go on feeling hopeless to change things, and spend a good deal of their future fortunes on little more than medical window dressing.

Get a clue! *You* decide how healthy you want to be. In rare cases will your genetics override you good habits. No more excuses for being unhealthy, tired, depressed, and unhappy. Let's re-learn basic nutrition, friends. The food producers and grocery stores will cater to our likes and dislikes. We have all the power if together we start eating smart again.

At least get this: The quality of your life and how much you will have to spend on health care from now until you die *greatly* depend on which foods you eat and don't eat on a daily basis. I highly recommend the book, *Skinny Bitch*, by Rory Freedman (former agent for Ford Models and self-taught know-it-all) and Kim Barnouin (former model, with Masters of Science in Holistic Nutrition). And oh, these women have a way with words!

$$$$$$$

Chapter 11

Those XXXXX Rich People

Okay, enough pot shots at the mad cow food industry. Let see if we can find some others to shake a big ugly stick at. It's always easier to blame someone else for our stupidity and financial messes, or some big monopoly company, or maybe even those *rich people themselves*.

How often do you hear some snide remark about rich people and how they mess things up for the rest of us? Comments like "rich people are the reason I can't get ahead, because they own and control everything." Or "rich people are greedy and just take money from the poor." Or "rich people don't pay their share in taxes." Maybe you've made comments like these before. I have.

Rich people, it turns out, are no guiltier of hurting us than the fast food giants or tobacco companies. After all, who is it that keeps forcing us to eat that super-sized, super fried Big Meal or some equally wicked food-stuff week after week, or perhaps day after day for some of us plus-sized eaters?

And who leads us down to the local quickie mart to buy cigarettes? To quote *Secrets of a Stingy Scoundrel* (Phil Villarreal) regarding these cancer sticks, "The tragedy isn't that cigarettes cause lung cancer; it's that they don't cause it fast enough. This isn't a wish, mind you, that all smokers would die, but just that they could see some tangible effects from their habit and have more of an impetus to fight it off."

Come on, no one is twisting our arm to do anything. *We* decide to do everything we do, including make a lot of stupid ass reckless decisions.

Yes, there *are* scammers just waiting for the kind of person who will leap before looking. By the way, if you've been scammed or are prone to being scammed, just do this simple trick: Before handing over any money or giving out any information to anyone, just tell them "I need to first ask my husband (or wife/family member/friend)." Then really go *ask* for someone else's opinion before you step in the dog doo.

Aside from scammers, some people are just trying to sell you what you want to buy. It's not their fault they are making money from us. It's our fault for willingly handing it over to them. Even if we're all just a bunch a big suckers, it's still not their fault.

We really should be asking ourselves just why we seem to have a problem with rich people. Is it simply penis envy because they have a bigger wad than us? Because I can guarantee you this: If you suddenly won a big lottery, I'm sure you'd change your attitude about being rich. That's because there's nothing wrong with being rich.

We shouldn't assume however, that just because someone has a lot of money that they obtained it by simply finagling others out of their money. It's nearly impossible to get rich by cheating others without a lot of planning and hard work. To be sure, we should all follow a rich person around for a week and see how they do it. We may be surprised at the long hours they put it and sacrifices they make to get there. They work hard for your money, damn it!

Okay, so assume for a minute that you're okay with people being rich. Should they be taxed more and pay more than their fair share just because they have money? You might want to rethink that too.

For starters, if the government decided to put a higher tax on rich peoples' toys (boats, limos, RVs, etc.) what do you think would happen? If I was a rich person, I'd shop around somewhere else for a better deal or just not buy the thing until later, because I got rich by being smart and I'm not going to pay any more taxes than I have to. So the equipment manufacturers will suffer decreased sales, and ultimately factory workers and sales people will lose jobs. So this tax on the rich backfires and Joe Worker is the one who actually suffers.

Or suppose I'm a millionaire business owner, and the government decides to raise my taxes because I'm rich. What do you think would happen? Yes, I'd technically pay the higher tax but ultimately my customers will pay it, since I'll just raise prices to cover the higher tax. After all, I didn't get rich by giving money away or losing my slim profit margin. So again, the tax on the rich backfires and Joe Consumer pays the tax instead. And if consumers won't pay the higher prices, then I'll just farm out my manufacturing to another country where wages are less. More local jobs lost.

Before you think how horrible it is that "rich" people will farm out labor out to another country, we consumers do the same sort of thing every day. We "farm out" our purchases. We want to find the best deal and often we won't even buy products made in our own country because they cost too much. When was the last time you looked at where something was made before you bought it? Remember my Raisin Bran? I bought it and brought it home, and in doing so helped finance farmed out groceries. I bet you do that every day too.

Okay, maybe these taxes on the rich really won't work but at least the rich should be paying their fair share of tax, right? Well, according to a surprising article, Why Taxing The Rich Doesn't Work (Gail Buckner), the top income earners really are paying their fair share. The top 1% of earners pay 40% of all taxes collected. Not only that, but the top income earners in the United States pay a larger share of the tax burden than their counterparts in any other industrialized country!

Again, it needs to be said: If *we* were the rich ones, our attitude would be a little different towards rich people. Think we can never get there? Well, if I never get rich I'm not going to blame rich people. They'll never stop <u>me</u> from getting rich. I can screw that up quite well on my own, thank you!

$$$$$$$

Chapter 12

You're Shrinking (That's What She Said)

There are tons of articles and blogs about the middle class' shrinking wealth while the rich are getting richer. That may be true, but did you ever stop and consider the possibility that the reason for this is that the middle class may just be getting stupider? For crap's sake, just look around at your friends and family and neighbors doing dumb ass things with money over and over again. So why, as much as we'd all love to, is the first assumption to blame rich people?

The fact that the middle class is getting poorer is not because rich people are taking our money. They're not taking my money. Why are they taking yours? I'm considered middle class too, yet I'm not poorer since the national financial fiascos starting in the first decade of the twenty first century. In fact, my wife and I bought a house at the height of the housing "bubble" and actually paid it off during the following recession.

We did initially lose nearly half of the money we had in the stock market. And our house value slumped. But when all this happened, we had no other debt but the mortgage, no car payments, no student loans, no credit card debt, or any other payments. Granted we were able to keep our jobs but we also continued to live cheap, drive older paid-for cars, and save. Any extra money we could squeeze out of each month's budget, we paid on our mortgage.

The stock market has made comebacks since it crashed big. And we continued to save since then. Bottom line, we did not end up poorer, but richer. It's all because of this: We finally wised up years ago about preventing others from taking our money (usually in the form of interest payments, but also in frivolous purchases).

Job losses, health issues, and other crises can bring on financial challenges, even disasters. But it doesn't always have to be the case. Some of these surprises do not have to wipe us out. With no debt, it is much, much easier to weather the storms.

If the rich are getting richer, it's only because they have figured out how to weather the storms. Understand this: Rich peoples' houses (if they are big and fancy) can drop in value a lot more than modest sized houses after a bubble bursts and are harder to sell. Rich people can lose money in a stock market crash just like the rest of us. They're not immune to economical disasters, usually they are just better prepared for them.

And that can be us, prepared for the bubble bursts, the job losses, the market dips, and other unexpected hits to our finances. The first thing to do is to <u>get out of debt</u>! It's surprising how little you can actually live on if you have no debt. It's also surprising how much money you can save if you have no debt. With no debt it feels like you're rich.

We know a young couple who has very little debt other than their mortgage. The husband lost his job nine months ago. His wife works just thirty hours per week. They can still make their house payment and even continue to save some money on one income because their debt level is so small.

Even better yet would be for all of us to pay off our mortgages. Can you imagine what that might feel like to have no mortgage? Of course you won't if you just rent and that gives a sense of freedom too. There is absolutely no shame in renting. Either way, do whatever it takes to shake off and shake down those payments and put money into savings every month.

Join the growing number of people who are playing a new game and setting their own rules. Getting out of debt is the only way to do it. Let's stop blaming the rich for making us poor, because it's really not them doing it.

Maybe the real blame is with our neighbors' Chihuahuas.

$$$$$$$

Chapter 13

My Neighbor's Dog, Foo Foo

Just how well do you get along with your neighbors? Does your neighbor's dog, Foo Foo, just bug the living crap out of you? Do you have evil thoughts about what you wish you could do to that little yapping maggot?

Okay, here's what not to do to your neighbor. My wife never laughed so hard. I was a fool and had to eat crow, wishing instead it was a barbeque mutt sandwich.

First you should know some background. Imagine this: our neighbors have two psychotic yappy Chihuahuas, who love nothing more than hanging out in the one location in their yard that happens to be right next to our bedroom window. Endless yapping at night, during the day, any time anything moves outside, whenever I walk in the yard, whenever I mow, all the bloody time! Oh, how I've been wishing they'd escape into our yard while I'm mowing or weed wacking. Did I mention midnight prayers for an "accident?"

Some more background. The front room of our house faces the street. Every morning we sit and have tea while waking up and looking out into the park across from our house. Inevitably, the morning dog walkers will stroll on down the sidewalk in front of our house with their Bonzos, Foo Foos and Ziggys. And like clockwork, the unwelcome little cockroaches take a steamer or wiz in the corner of our yard by the light pole.

No matter what thorny brush or prickly shrub we transplant to that light pole area, or secret concoction we spray there, it seems like every dog that passes by is so interested in that bloody corner. And I refuse to provide the neighborhood doggie toilet!

On more than one occasion we've opened the window and yelled something during a morning dump and embarrassed the owner. It has become a source of irritation for us, far worse than our kid's most obnoxious banging, clanging, talking toy.

So imagine my surprise one afternoon as I'm sitting in the front room at the computer sipping my glorious afternoon tea. I see the neighbor clamoring by with the two psycho Chihuahuas. And, yep, like clockwork they stop at the blessed corner. "Oh, no you don't!" I thought. And like a dog taking a determined dump on the weedy lawn in the background of a redneck wedding ceremony, I see the classic canine mini-squat in slow motion. Sure enough, a fresh steaming deposit, albeit small. I should not have been surprised that he just let it do its business right there but I was.

The dog's owner, our neighbor, looked up towards our house and, I could see by the look on his face exactly what he was thinking, "Is anyone looking?" He gazed again toward the house. "No, great," he must have thought. Of course, he couldn't see that I was seething at the whole thing. So after Foo Foo did his thing, the owner nonchalantly proceeds to walk his snarling little poop machines down the sidewalk.

Now we all know the "do unto others as you would have them do unto you" routine, so being the church-goer that I am, I decided to do unto him. I should say, "doo" unto him. Immediately I proceeded to our garage, hit the garage opener button, and grabbed a shovel. I wasn't mad, just determined, with one goal in mind – to return the pile to its rightful owner.

50

Of course, I don't really relish confrontation, and by then the neighbor was probably fifty yards down the street. I instantly found the foul belongings, scooped them up purposefully, and then marched up the sidewalk towards the neighbor's driveway.

On a side note, in our youth my brothers and I had been quite fond of the gasoline, dog doo, and bag trick – you know, light the bag of dog doo on fire on someone's door step, ring the doorbell and run! The surprise is *after* the fire is stomped out! Yes, that crossed my mind. But with our neighbor I just wanted to get even, not create an ongoing feud. So I just deposited the soft chunks, three of them, on his driveway.

After putting the shovel away and returning inside the house, I told my wife the whole sequence of events. She seemed quite taken with my story and laughed quite heartily. Proud of myself, I returned to the front room and the computer.

Not paying attention to the time, maybe ten minutes had passed and I happened to glance up from the computer and look out the window. I was very surprised to the neighbor again. But this time, with Foo Foo and Cookie nosing about, he was hunched over looking for something in that famous corner of my yard. Eyeing, scanning. Oh, I wish I would have thought to get out my camera to get that face! The surprised look of confusion was so classic.

But what's that? A bag in his hand? "Ahhh, you're kidding," I thought. "You actually came back with a bag to pick it up?" Now that was one thing I *didn't* see coming.

On another side note, you know how dog owners will scoop up the treasure and then turn the bag inside out around their hand like some sort of sick puppet?

And then put it in their pocket afterwards? Have you seen that? Gotta love dog lovers. They don't mind finishing their walk with a gushy sack of nasty in their belly pack, just waiting to ooze out!

But I diverge. Back to our neighbor. He was quite intent on finding the stash and looking a little taken aback as to where it must be! "I knew it was here," I could just hear him thinking. He crouched and waved his hand puppet around and looked some more, scanning back a third time. He finally gave up and continued walking up the sidewalk towards his house.

Busted! By now, I ran to the other room to tell my wife again of this bizarre sequence of events. She laughed even harder, knowing that the neighbor would discover that I had left some presents for him on his driveway! Ahhhh!

Now what to do? Do I just figure, "Heck with it, he got what he deserved?" when in actuality he had already made amends for the mutt, at least in intent. Hmm. I just went back to the computer and shrugged it off. Another ten minutes or so had passed, maybe a half hour. Then I heard my wife telling our five year old that "Papa should go apologize." Not thirty seconds later our daughter comes into the front room to tell me, "You should go apologize."

At first I thought, "naaa" no need, no big deal. But I did feel a little guilty about the whole thing. And I realized how this could forever change the dynamic between our neighbors and us. All over some stupid thing, those blasted little mutts. So I swallowed my pride and set out on the long trip up the sidewalk. As I reached their driveway I noticed that my presents were no longer there. Stepping up to the front door, I pressed my finger on the doorbell switch. Gulp…

This story was used with permission from the idiot who had the gall to mess with his neighbor like that. While I can't claim to have any better manners, I bet my yard looks better than his, especially since his neighbor probably got revenge.

$$$$$$$

Chapter 14

Stress and Dynamite

Okay, if inheritances gone AWOL, payday stores, your junk food addictions, mega foods companies, rich people, or your neighbors' dogs aren't really the causes of your financial downfalls, then maybe stress is paralyzing you.

We have all probably read stories about how too much stress (or being unhappy) has negative health effects, emotionally and physically. Continual anxiety and discontent can lead to mental exhaustion, depression, eating disorders, dietary issues, a weakened immune system, and other physical illnesses that can even contribute to premature death. We also know that unhealthy stresses can be dramatically increased by poor sleeping habits, lack of proper nutrition, and inadequate exercise.

But do we ever think that our numb nut money habits may be the major contributor to our higher tension level? The point is, stress is going to cost you financially because of its effect on your health. In fact, whether you like it or not, at some point your biggest expenses are going to be to deal with your medical issues. If stress is wreaking havoc, then we need to get at the root and pull that sucker out now.

"The biggest nerve in the human body is the one to the wallet." Sorry, I don't know the author of this statement but I heard a preacher say this one time and it rang true. The fact is that we get emotional about money. And I would bet that more often than not, that emotion comes out as an unhealthy worry.

Unless our money situation is ideal, we're going to tend to be bothered about it, at least a little. The sad truth is that too many people are in tough financial shape and it is adding a mountain of pressure to our lives. And this has a definite health consequence, not to mention its effects on our marriages, jobs, and everyday life.

So what do we do about this? It's tough if you lose your job and find yourself upside down on your home. And it's also difficult to keep ending up with too much month left at the end of the money, even when you're working hard.

Here's the thing. The tougher financial spot you're in, the more radical you're going to have to get to escape the pressure cooker. You're going to need some dynamite. Maybe it's time to consider:

Renting for a while longer, instead of buying a house,

Selling the house and renting instead,

Moving to a less expensive area,

Selling the house and buying a smaller house,

Selling a car that has a loan balance, paying off the upside portion and buying an older vehicle with cash,

Selling the big rig and getting a smaller one,

Selling the boat,

Selling the camper,

Buying used stuff instead of buying it new,

Renting stuff instead of buying it (campers, boats, tools),

Selling anything you don't use or need,

Selling anything that has a payment and getting rid of the payment,

Selling *everything* and starting over!!!

From my experience, most people don't want to get radical enough. Most people prefer to stay with familiar problems rather than find solutions that may create brief havoc in their life, even though their money behaviors are causing much more havoc. This is nuts. If your feet outgrew your shoes, then you'd replace the shoes, even if the new pair felt stiff and uncomfortable for a bit.

So why continue to struggle month after month in other areas of your life? Would you be willing to do any of the above things if that's what it took to de-stress? You can always buy things later when you are no longer struggling. Yes, it can be very hard to let go of stuff. But once you start doing it, it becomes very liberating because you start to feel the fog lifting.

So go for it. Get radical. Get fighting mad. Get fucking mad. Light the dynamite fuse. Wriggle your way out of debt as fast as you can. Sell whatever you have to. You'll find a lot of peace at the end of the road. And you'll be amazed at how much less stress you have in your life. It feels so good, and it's good for you. How many things can you say that about!

But remember, it's not just about feeling good. It's about being healthier. And that translates to more money that you'll keep in your pocket and not given up to some dip wad poser doctor or his pharmaceutical scam partner in crime.

$$$$$$$

Chapter 15

That Hated Little Pink Piggy

Well, I don't want to leave the stress discussion before giving you another story about a fun way to relieve stressors. You break them! Beware though, your child may cry if you do something like this.

That hated little pink piggy. Maybe "hate" is too strong of a word. But annoying just doesn't do it justice. Either way, anyone who has ever had kids or been around kids probably has a personal experience with a toy that drove them crazy.

You know, that noisy, squeaky, repetitive, grate-on-your-nerves wonder toy that the TV glamorized, your child had to have, and now you are stuck listening to, with the stark reality of waiting for the blasted thing to break while secretly hoping you could drop kick it over the neighbor's fence.

That being said, one of our "favorite" such toys was this little pink, fuzzy, cutesy, singing porky pig with motorized legs. Our five year old daughter "won" the bloody thing at a Christmas white elephant gift exchange. Sounds harmless enough, huh? But if that's all there was to it, I wouldn't be writing this. At its evil core was that song.

Granted, it sang a rather nice Christmas tune. Or rather, *normally* it would be a nice Christmas tune. And I have absolutely nothing against Christmas jingles. But the song was recorded with the most aggravating cutesy voice and intertwined with the most grating pig snorts and grunts, which continued all the way through the song! Aside from the fact that one could take offense at what may seem like a mockery of a Christmas song, the overall effect was just plain irritating no matter what the song might have been.

So our daughter quickly learned of our displeasure with this toy, though she continued to love it. In fact, she seemed to take pleasure in bringing it out into our presence and pressing that little button on the pig's ear to watch <u>us</u> squirm. And that was its undoing.

On one such occasion my wife and I were in the kitchen cooking and our daughter was pestering us for something and didn't like our answer. So she promptly said "hmm" and went and got little piggy, placed it on the kitchen counter, pressed the start button on its ear, and walked away!

As soon as those oh-too-familiar harassing sounds began to pummel us, my wife swiftly reached over and nabbed it off of the counter and placed it high on top of our refrigerator. The trouble is, that blasted pig's legs were motoring about as it sang and pranced and within a few moments we both glanced up and saw piggy teetered towards the edge.

My wife and I looked quickly at each other and our eyes were saying, "Are you going to jump to catch it?" I'm sure we both thought "naaaa" at the same time as we watched the little pink blob do a side roll off the front edge of the frig. Like a swimmer's diving nightmare, little pig landed squarely on its side on the tile floor with a slight snapping sound. And all was a blessed quiet!

As my wife and I grinned at each other, our daughter, who had heard the thump and ran back into the room, burst into tears. We had to turn our heads away to hide the uncontrollable snickering at this neat stroke of luck.

As Dr. Seuss asked many decades ago in his book *The Cat In The Hat*, "What would *you* do?" Hey, accidents do happen after all.

$$$$$$$

Chapter 16

The Debt Rant

"I don't care, I love it," so the song goes about crashing a car into a bridge. Well, I've done that before too, literally with a car and figuratively with debt. I must have loved it too. And if you love debt, then you will probably lose out on millions like I did. What's wrong with a little debt? Everything!

Do you realize that many people have not read a non-fiction book since high school? In contrast, I've heard that millionaires typically read several non-fiction books every month. Hmm, does it really make a difference? Let's see. Which will make me smarter, books about real shit or the television and radio drivel? Da!

Why do we keep falling for the "You've arrived if you own this or drive this" pitches? Are we really that frickin' stupid? Maybe we are. When it comes to money, there's little sound advice on television or the radio.

Most of what is said on the television and radio about money is a scam, a lie, deceitful outright bullshit, not wise, and designed to keep us in bondage. To make us want to buy, buy, buy. To make us slaves to the banks and to our stuff. *That* is why Americans are in so much debt. We've fallen for very good marketing and even grander lies.

We've been trained, and I hesitate to say brainwashed lest you think I'm just paranoid, that this is how you "get ahead." You borrow for anything and everything you want. Don't wait, don't save, don't sacrifice. Have it all now. Have more than our grandparents ever did before we're half their age! And if we get in over our heads, hey, just file for bankruptcy and walk away. Pass it on to our kids and grandkids to clean up.

Come on people, let's wake up! Is life really so hopeless that we spend our money like tomorrow won't happen? Or do we just not care about tomorrow? Either way we shouldn't expect the government to fix our stupidity like an enabling parent. Where do you think their money comes from anyway? *We* pay for all government bailouts one way or another.

Debt is unintelligent and the surest way for you to be a broke and powerless moron. Debt is killing us. Please, let's stop doing it now. How many second chances will we get?

$$$$$$$

Chapter 17

The Pyramid Scheme of Banking

This is a little different spin on why so many of us are in debt: Most of us are at the bottom of several pyramid schemes at any given time in our lives.

Recently, I reread the book *"The Freedom Bell Curve"* by Robert Minteer. The author makes a strong case for why most businesses and institutions function like a pyramid scheme, economically enslaving the people at the bottom. Of course, most of us are there by choice, but that's beside the point.

In his book, what he terms the "Topsoppers," those at the top of the pyramid scheme of power, derive their power from the "Mopsoppers" (those companies and individuals caught on the corporate ladders trying to work their way up) and the "Boppers" (those at the bottom working like slaves and hoping to someday "arrive" at a Mopsopper standard of living).

Whether it's the government, the legal and medical professions, insurance "industry" (though they produce nothing), the banking establishments or any number of other big businesses making up the Topsopper and Mopsopper organizations, their success and riches come to a large extent at the expense and hard work of the Boppers who make up the common factory line worker, tradesperson, craftsman, burger flipper, and cubicle geek. The majority of those who buy all consumer products are Boppers, often borrowing money to do so.

The Topsoppers and Mopsoppers are always at varying times acting as the middlemen in trading, setting the prices and terms. Minteer says, "In any trading, when the terms of the trade fluctuate, one trader gains and the other loses – but the middleman always gains." The ones who lose are most often the Boppers, the workers at the bottom who are also the biggest consumers. The system is set up against us. And the banks play a large role in helping things stay that way.

What, you don't like this legalized pyramid extortion system and being a gullible Bopper at the bottom helping to make everyone above richer? Then get the hell out.

$$$$$$$

Chapter 18

Do We Really Need Banks?

What have banks really done for us other than, like the toughest most badass prison cell mate, make us bend over and pick up the soap in the shower? That sums it up pretty well, don't ya think?

The banks make money by paying us a token interest rate on our deposits, and then loaning them out at a much higher interest rate. They *need* us to make money. Yet, at least at the time of writing this book, it's an insult what banks are paying as savings account interest rates – a fraction of one percent! It amounts to nothing for the average person who saves.

The banks make money by practicing fractional reserve lending whereby they in effect can loan out ten times the amount of actual deposits that they have on hand. But what if all the depositors want their money all at once (it has happened before, and will surely happen again)? No problem, you say, the banks are insured through the Federal Deposit Insurance Corporation (FDIC). Indeed they are. But do you want to try to get your money back from the government during a crisis? The government will first bail out the Big Boys before worrying about the bottom feeders.

Even without your borrowing, the banks make a killing from the average "customer" by charging fees and penalties. A few bucks from everyone, month after month. It's robbery. Less and less people are saving money so the banks have resorted to clever shakedown tactics.

The banks (including credit card companies) encourage the average consumer to borrow and borrow, though it is frickin' stupid advice. They want to keep us in bondage, ever paying back interest and provide a steady income for them.

So the basic obvious question is this: What good to us is our money in a bank and why do we use banks for anything? We're getting paid squat for interest. In a crisis we may not get our money (especially in a timely manner) so it's not necessarily safe or liquid. And in reality we're losing money just to keep it there or do business with them.

We need to begin the process of ceasing our support to such institutions. The first and most important thing to do is to get out of debt by any means possible, by selling stuff, downsizing, selling everything if necessary and starting over, and working overtime or extra jobs.

Then, strongly consider whether you need a bank for anything. Do you *really* need your credit card or debit card? You can survive without a checking account. Do you need the bank's "great" interest payments on your savings account? Do you need their hassle? Seriously, what good are they? *Have you made more from them than they have taken from you?*

Cash is king, folks, and always has been. The banks (and others) have lied to us to get us to stop using cash and coins. It's harder for them to track our spending habits if we use cash.

Might our spare money, our cash and coin, do just as well under our pillows, in our mattresses, or in our home safe? You can find a bargain on a home safe on Craigslist. Or you can find some other safe place to stash your stash. I'm only half kidding about this.

If you're not willing to quit using banks altogether, continuing to deposit your paychecks and save your money there, at least quit borrowing money from them.

$$$$$$$

Chapter 19

Your Stupid Payment Plan

Oh, debt deserves so much more ranting and raving. If you're seeing a common theme in some of these chapters, it's intentional. If I could hit you with a big knurly get out of debt stick to keep you from losing your millions, I would.

Many money topics seem like common sense. But if they really are, why do people act like they've had a brain enema? Take payments for example (take them, please!). When buying stuff, big or small, why is it all about whether we can afford the bloody payment?

On our biggest life purchase, our house, whether we can afford it or not comes down to what the monthly payment will be. The monthly payment limits our purchase, not the purchase price. Hmm…so we usually overpay and stretch out the payments as long as possible.

Even for one of our next largest expenditures, our vehicle(s), it's the same thing. It's not the purchase price that limits how much we spend usually, but the monthly payment. Go figure. So we buy more than we can afford and stretch the payments longer.

And it continues likewise on down the line to smaller things like appliances, furniture, televisions, and other stuff we just have to have. It's too often not the purchase price that determines whether we'll buy it, but ultimately the monthly payment.

Jane, you ignorant slut. We've been cleverly marketed to and "trained" to think in terms of payments, not how much out-of-pocket it's going to cost when we finally pay it off. Have you ever added up all the interest you're paying to banks and credit card companies every month?

If you're like many people with a mortgage, car payments, credit card debt, and student loans, I've estimated that there is a good chance you're paying up to $1000 per month *in interest alone*. That is why the bank has a huge fancy building with high-end furniture, while you boast a double wide mobile home with particle board furniture. No wonder you can't seem to get ahead.

The solution is bone-headed simple: CASH. If you only used cash to make purchases (checks are fine too, if you have the money to cover them), you would evaluate each purchase based on how much it cost, or hurt, to dip into that pile. With cash we would save so much money on items because we wouldn't be paying interest, we would shop around more to get the best price, and fear of depleting our cash reserves would scare us off from even making some purchases to begin with.

That's why cash rocks. You spend less, or not at all sometimes. And while you're waiting to make a purchase, someone *pays you* to hold your money, albeit not much but that's a different problem. Cool. So now let's make "payment" a word from a foreign language. Let's boot-kick that fucker back to the bank where it belongs.

Still In The Red

You're still in the red
And feeling quite blue
Your money's still leaving
With your sanity too

So come to your senses
Get out of debt
Your banker won't thank you
Your wife will I bet

Then hope's on the horizon
While growing your stash
Your life's getting grand
Even better with cash

But you're still in the red
Your neighbor blue too
A smack on your heads
May be all we can do

$$$$$$$

74

Chapter 20

Student Loan Shams

We know how expensive it is to go to college, especially if you have a family and other financial obligations. But that's still no excuse to go overboard with student loans. Avoid student loans like your neighbor's snarling, frothy-mouthed pit bull. They bite in more ways than one.

If you *have* to borrow money for college, then pick the most financially affordable school. The truth is, with few exceptions, the school you attend will have little impact on what you learn, the job you get, or how much you will make when you graduate. Don't fool yourself into thinking it's all about the school. It's not. Only snobs think it is. Instead it's all about what you get out of it and your personal motivation. Employers won't care as much about the school as they do your character and the fact that you have the degree.

Don't borrow money for college just so you don't have to work while you're getting your degree. Talk about a lazy ass. If you can't do school with only minimal loans throughout (or better yet, none), then you need to work more, sell a lot of your stuff, and/or live cheaper. You, the student, may have to work full-time and go to school. You are correct, working and going to school stinks more than a bucket full of assholes. But so does a butt load of debt that never seems to go away.

Most student loans (if guaranteed by the government) will not go away in a bankruptcy. You'll be stuck with those for life. Is the savings in interest rates really worth the added risk? If you simply must borrow money for school, then get it through some other means than traditional student loans. The interest rate may be higher but there is less risk to your financial future.

If you do borrow money you'll be tempted to defer payments for a while after you graduate from college. After all, you'll want to buy other things like a house, some fancy new vehicles, and other toys to show the world you've arrived. Deferring your student loans is another big dumb shit financial mistake though. Don't do it. The interest will just keep on compounding and make the amount owed grow larger and larger to match the size of your stupid gland.

If you can't afford to pay back your student loans right away (as in a year or two, maximum, after graduating) then you really can't afford to get them in the first place.

So, to recap: DO pick an affordable school, do work while you go to school and "pay as you go" no matter if it takes a few years longer, and if you get loans for school do pay them back within a year or two maximum after graduating.

DON'T pick a fancy school just because it would be "cool" to go there or for some other snob factor, don't be a student only (work too), if you get loans don't get "student loans" but some other type of loan, and if you get loans don't defer loan payments until long after you graduate.

$$\$\$\$\$\$\$\$$$

Chapter 21

One Quick Thought on the "B' Word

The Budgeting topic has been bludgeoned enough elsewhere so I will refrain from a tirade in this book. But I believe a budget is *key* to your success with money. It's the key to your millions, really.

Just get this: Every dollar lost out of your wallet now is another one, or two, or ten that has to be earned again before you can kick you job to the curb. So learn to budget every month and shave off years of having to set your alarm clock. Budgeting is not necessarily fun and glamorous, but I bet your job is not a barrel of peeing monkeys either.

$$$$$$$

Chapter 22

Forever A Mobile Home

Since your home is probably going to be the biggest purchase you ever make in your life and perhaps your largest stumbling block to ever becoming a millionaire if you insist on doing it in a stupid fashion, the topic of houses, mortgages, tax write offs, and some the crappy myths deserve more than a little lip service. If fact, they deserve a smack in the face. So let's start with the most detestable of purchases in this area.

Trailers, mobile homes, and manufactured houses rotting in those trailer parks and mobile manors – they all bite like a rabid dog, a smelly bog, a crusty hog, or a gooey brown log. Feel my love?

Seems like every state, every county, and every town is littered with a "shady grove" mobile home manor. I'm not criticizing the folks who live in mobile homes. Some of our best friends do. And I've lived in mobile homes more than once in my life, from an old crusty 1949 bullet blasted, hand-painted two-tone twenty four foot long Shultz during college, to a slightly newer single wide when I first got married, to a newer doublewide that hurt my pride and my wallet because I should have known better.

I despise mobile homes now because they had something to do with me not seeing my first million.

Sure, if I was lucky enough to be able to buy a lot with an ocean view with a mobile home on it, I'd live in it for a while. But for everyday living, you're throwing a lot of money away. There is no advantage, cost or otherwise, to living in a mobile home.

They depreciate like a car, and end up looking like they belong in a junk yard. You're better off renting to save the extra money. Then you don't have to spend it on lot rent, mortgage interest, taxes, insurance, and maintenance. Then when you can afford it, buy a real house that appreciates in value.

Don't make one of these factory assembly line jokes the reason you never see your lucky million. Please, try like hell to get out of a mobile home or else you'll look and feel like you're there already. You and your neighborhood will, however, have the perfect backdrop for a super scary Halloween so I guess it's not all loss.

$$\$\$\$\$\$\$\$$$

Chapter 23

Duped By The Property Ladder

There's a big ass lie being sold on some of those fun TV shows. It's marketed by banks and endorsed by government tax write offs. And we've fallen for it big time. If you get nothing else from this book, please take to heart my rantings about debt and about purchasing homes.

We have fallen for the line that houses are a "great investment." And if you can qualify for a loan you should buy the biggest, nicest one you can "afford" so you don't keep throwing your money away on rent. And then once you're a home "owner," keep trading up and moving up the property ladder. Eventually, you'll be the master of your very own mansion.

More like masturbator in a trailer park. Give me a break! Playing the property ladder game is a sure way to the poor house. There is no disgrace in renting, or at least renting longer, and it is not throwing money away.

Come on numb chucks, do you throw your money away when you buy necessities like groceries, clothes for your kids, or health insurance? No. You have to pay for things to live, including your shelter, one way or another. That's just the way it is.

Your shelter is going to cost, and it's just a matter of who you are paying – the rental owner or the bank and government. And you'll probably always pay more to the latter (or the "ladder," however you want to look at it).

If you rent you have pretty low risk. But if you buy, then you have to pay the property taxes, insurance, and maintenance. Plus, if you buy a house with a loan, you're going to pay the bank's extortion, and keep paying for decades unless you decide to wise up.

If you do buy a house, here's how to be smart about it. Put at least a 20% down payment on it (or whatever amount eliminates the need for mortgage insurance, which by the way protects only the bank, not you). The best policy is 100% down payment. But most of us won't wait until we save the full amount, so just make sure the down payment is sizeable. Then, pay off the loan in ten years or less. Less is better.

If you can't put at least 20% down and pay the house off in ten years or less, then you are buying too much house and/or paying too much. So shop around. Wait. Downsize it. Look in a cheaper area. Resist house fever. Your peace of mind later is worth resisting the impulse to buy your worst nightmare now.

$$$$$$$

Chapter 24

Tiny Two Tango Bathrooms

"But I want it!" Get over it, ass breath, you can't afford it. And by the way, did anyone ever tell you that your breath could knock a buzzard off a shit wagon?

Ahem. My wife and I really do enjoy watching those TV shows where people are looking for a house to purchase. Their wish lists and desired house sizes are usually much bigger than their budgets. But you do have to admire their huge balls in making Americans look like a bunch of spoiled whiners. Among many of their disappointed scowls, they always turn up their noses at any bathroom that is small, especially if it only has one sink. They want a spa bathroom and think they can't do with less. They should.

Buying too much house is the biggest mistake people make. They buy as much house as they're qualified to borrow the money for and not what they can really afford. Then it takes them way too long to pay it off. Our rule is to buy only as much house as you can pay off in ten years or less.

That may mean a smaller bathroom, with only one sink as well. What's wrong with that? People think it's impossible to share a bathroom while getting ready in the morning.

My wife and I have been sharing a small, one-sink bathroom every morning, no problem, for almost nine years. Our house has been paid off for almost three years. So stick that up your Jacuzzi.

Take your pick: Small bathroom and affordable sized house, or spa bathroom with the big house and be the bank's little whore.

$$$$$$$

Chapter 25

Duped By The Tax Write Off

And your big pie hole is saying, "But I get such a good tax write off if I buy a big house and have a big mortgage." Fine, go have a threesome with your banker and Uncle Sam and get reamed from both sides.

A lot of people brag about their "great tax write-off." I snicker. Don't get me wrong, if you are buying something because you need it and get a tax deduction on the side, that's great. But when your decision to buy something is swayed because you'll get the tax advantage, well, that's laughable and sad. This isn't even elementary school level math, or logic. You're spending a dollar to save a quarter.

One of the most common and largest tax write-offs for the average person or family is associated with the home mortgage. The interest is usually tax deductible. No one seems to do the math, though. I know of too many people who won't pay off their house early because of the tax deduction, or just as bad, buy too much house because of the tax deduction.

Because of not crunching the numbers, people will pay the bank a dollar just to save a quarter on taxes. And they will lose seventy-five cents of every dollar they pay to interest! So why would anyone justify keeping a mortgage any longer than necessary or buying more house than they need just because they can write off the interest? The answer is, we've been duped. And we've bought the trick like a two-bit Shanghai whore.

As if paying a dollar to save a quarter isn't bad enough, if you have a mortgage you'll have to pay quite a bit in interest (and/or other deductions) before you even exceed the "standard" tax deduction to make it worth the bother. The standard deduction is quite a sizeable benefit. Did you get this? You have a choice every year to either take the standard tax deduction or itemize your deductions (basically just adding up mortgage interest, property tax, giving to charities, etc.).

You can take the standard deduction even if you have no mortgage or any other deductions, but if you itemize you'll have to exceed this amount before it does any good. Unless your mortgage interest and other deductions exceed the standard deduction, you get nothing for all the pain. Why would anyone want to pay that much in interest when you already get a free standard deduction? The answer is, we've been Shanghai'd again.

Don't even get me started on houses and the fact that they're rarely a good investment when you have a mortgage (I'm not against houses, just against buying them like you're retarded).

Tax write-offs are just an incentive to buy, and more often by using credit. They were not created with you in mind, but were created with "others grabbing your money" in mind. We don't just fall for this in buying houses either. We may buy all kinds of stuff for our businesses too (vehicles, furniture, electronics, appliances, tools, etc.), thinking that the tax savings make it a good bargain. On the surface it does look like a bargain.

Buying a bargain you don't really need isn't saving you anything. Just look at those matching his and hers sunflower yellow knit sweaters in your closet. Oh what a steal.

Don't let your tax write-offs be the reason you buy anything. Get stuff you need, yes, and take the tax deduction if it's there. But if you can, avoid even being eligible for tax write offs.

If you simply don't want to take this advice and "have to" have a tax deduction, here's the best one: Give to charity! You'll get the same tax deduction. You'll still spend a dollar to save a quarter. But this time the dollar goes to a worthy cause, not to increase the bank's profit. And you get paid back a quarter in tax savings for being so nice. Now *there* is a good incentive.

$$$$$$$

Chapter 26

Smart Tax Write Offs

If you want to have a bunch of tax write offs every year, at least pull your head out of your ass and understand how to be more effective with them.

We pretty much give it all to Caesar (our beloved government) until April or May or beyond each year, right? So here's a thought. Be a Ceaser instead! Stop paying so much. We're not saying quit paying taxes. Just quit paying more than you have to.

Here's a trick that I wish I'd learned many years ago because it could have saved me a shit load on taxes. This isn't talked about a lot. And ironically, it was one of my $19.95 home tax software programs that recommended it.

If you give money to charities or other causes that are tax deductible and/or have other deductions (such as mortgage interest, property tax, other taxes) that are sufficient enough to push you from taking a standard deduction on your tax return to itemizing these things, then here is the trick.

After you have given/paid these tax deductible things throughout the year, if you have the extra cash, then give/pay next year's items too in December. In fact, plan to have the extra cash to do this. That way when you file your taxes you'll have a whole heap more tax deductible items.

Then the following year, take the standard deduction. Since you will have given/paid most or all of that year's items the previous December, it's likely that the standard deduction will be by far greater than whatever tax deductible items are left for that year.

Get it? You itemize one year and take the standard deduction the next. Then itemize the next, standard deduction the next and so on. It's not rocket science. The years you itemize you always do two years' worth of deductible giving, interest, and other taxes if you can. You could save thousands with just a little planning.

But do the math first. Plan it all out to determine just what the savings will be. Yes, it will require some not-so-fun digging through your tax records. Frankly, I'd rather dig through the dumpster at a rogue dairy farm. But you really could save big for your efforts. Once you figure it out the first time and have a plan, it will be relatively easy after that.

Just think of the possibilities of not giving it all to the government. You could put it towards your first million. Or maybe some causes near and dear to your heart can benefit instead.

$$$$$$$

Chapter 27

Will You Be Forced To Do This?

To all homeowners who haven't planned enough for retirement: Beware of the winking marauders who look like your favorite has-been actors.

Perhaps you've heard of the claimed benefits of reverse mortgages to help you out in retirement if you're short on monthly income. And after all, these products are endorsed by more than one glib and graying over-the-hill actor so they must be good, right?

You know the drill: Get a reverse mortgage and have no more mortgage payments! All it takes is being at least sixty-two years old and an easy government-insured loan against your home equity. You receive a lump sum or monthly payments for years to come and get to live in your house too. Easy money!

I'm not here to say that reverse mortgages are some great evil. Hell, maybe they are. At a minimum they do seem a bit devious. I've always been leery. For some reason, a red flag goes off every time I see one of those poker face ads.

With a reverse mortgage you greatly increase the risk that you, your spouse, or your family will get into financial hot water down the road. Obviously, someone wouldn't consider a reverse mortgage unless they were a little strapped for income in the first place. First big red flag! Who are they targeting? Don't those pesky payday loan store thieves target people who can least afford it too? Hmm…

So basically, because we need extra money to live on we are going to borrow it using our house as security,

right? Stu-pid. That's what stolen credit cards are for!
But really, when does borrowing money to live on ever
make sense? At some point, especially if you did this at
a relatively young age, you will run out of money. Then
what? Eventually it ALL has to be paid back, with
interest and fees. Is your house really going to
appreciate enough to keep up with all that?

You are still responsible for paying the insurance,
taxes, and maintenance on your home after getting a
reverse mortgage. So is it possible or even probable,
being so short of cash in the first place, that you may not
be able to make some of the insurance or tax payments
along the way? I read an interesting article in
Kiplinger's Personal Finance that reported that 9% of
reverse mortgage borrowers were at risk of foreclosure
because they were behind on tax and insurance bills.
Another red flag. Ouch!

Is it also possible that you may become a slacker in
doing all the necessary house maintenance since you're
on a tight budget? If maintenance was neglected for
many years (since to keep the house it will always be a
priority to pay taxes and insurance first), then so much
more money will be lost when your house is eventually
sold. Whose loss will this be? The bank's loss? No, it
will be your spouse's or family's loss more likely.

And then the final red flag is the cost of the loan
itself. These are expensive, ugly loans, much worse
than a loan from the scar faced loan shark who fell from
an ugly tree and hit every branch on the way down. If
you don't run from these loans, you'll be paying for an
upfront insurance premium (up to 2% of the value of the
home, regardless of how much you borrow), loan
origination fees (some up to $6000), traditional closing
costs like appraisals and title searches, and other

monthly service fees that will rob a huge amount of money from your home equity right off the top.

Don't forget: Any time you have a bank or lending institution "help" you with money you can guarantee that they will profit at your expense. That's just how the scummy bastards work.

Given the costs of the reverse mortgage loan, your home insurance, property taxes, and required maintenance, how can you possibly come out ahead? You can't, unless the housing market in your area is so hot (or is hot at the time the loan needs paying back). Can you ever be sure of the housing market? This is not something I would want to gamble my largest asset on at any age. But if you do take the gamble, the lender will profit handsomely up front, and that's really what's driving this whole push on reverse mortgages. Someone wants their coffers filled, and to ream you in the process.

So before being tempted by a reverse mortgage, please consider that you would likely be far better off financially, with more peace of mind and with much lower risk, to simply sell your house and rent a nice little downsized house or apartment. You can take the profit from the sale of your home, bank it or invest it in something low risk and still draw off a nice steady income for much longer.

As I've said many times, there is no shame in renting. And living without debt is so much more peaceful. That's what I want in my old age.

$$$$$$$

Chapter 28

Bull's Eye On Your Back

At the risk of offending some of my family and friends, I'm going to throw this out there. Do snake oil sellers see you coming? Are you a scam target? Do you have a big "kick me in the ass" sign taped on your backside?

The topic of scams really deserves a little raging, because you'll definitely have trouble getting to millionaire status if you can't resist a good scam line.

Recently I attended a seminar called "Spot the Red Flags of Fraud" hosted by the Financial Industry Regulatory Authority (FINRA). It was great. Ironically, in the middle of the seminar, I got a pre-recorded spam marketing call on my cell phone trying to get me to sign up for some rip off web service.

It seems that everywhere, every day, we are bombarded with "offers" to help us or make us richer, yet designed to squeeze some blood from a turnip. Personally, I have no trouble quickly deleting such messages from my computer or phone, laughing at the hideous TV ads, or even being a little rude on the phone if I actually get a live person trying to get my money. But many people are a little too nice when it comes to allowing a cleverly designed sales scheme, pitched by a nice sounding salesperson to take hold of their emotions.

Here are some of the lines you may hear, all designed to snag you into their web.

How would you like to make some easy money? Run! There is really no such thing. Success takes planning, time, and hard work.

This investment opportunity is risk free (or has a guaranteed return). Do not be fooled. Investments are never risk free and guaranteed returns have conditions.

This product is available for a limited time only. Do not fall for it. They'll be more than glad to take your money next week or next month just the same.

Everyone is trying to get in on this (or many of your neighbors, co-workers, or family and friends are doing it). So what! Just because all your neighbors are jumping off a cliff, why should you? Consider this: The majority of people are not doing so good financially, so do not copy them!

The sales associate looks/sounds so professional. So does Satan.

As the old saying goes, if it sounds too good to be true then it probably blows chunks.

Okay, so we're all safe from these pickup lines, right? After all, it is usually just unsophisticated, uneducated schmucks who fall for this, right? Wrong. According to FINRA, here's the demographic that falls for such lines the most:

Male,

Married,

55 to 65 years old,

Financially literate,

College educated,

Self-reliant,

Recent change in financial health (or way "behind the curve" financially with lots of time to make up for),

Risk takers (always open to new investment opportunities),

Already owns high risk investments,

Relies on family and friends for financial advice,

Fails to check the background or registration status of products/sellers.

Sound like any losers you know? We know many duds who fit this mold too.

Here are a few tricks to avoid being scammed: Ask questions, such as "Are you licensed to sell this product and is the product registered?" and then verify it. Avoid "free dinner" type presentations that make you feel an obligation to reciprocate since you received something. Avoid high risk investments. Get second and third opinions in the investment, not from family and friends but from professionals (not salespersons) in the field. Develop a "refusal script" for when you get calls or are approached with the "opportunity."

Protect the ass that took you years to develop and grow! For more information, try these very useful resources:

Save And Invest http://www.saveandinvest.org/
Free Movie, *Tricks of the Trade*
http://www.saveandinvest.org/FraudCenter/P124313
Financial Industry Regulatory Authority
http://www.finra.org/

Washington State Department of Financial Institutions http://www.dfi.wa.gov/ (find similar website for your state)

$$$$$$$

Chapter 29

Invest With Uncle Pete?

Has a family member ever approached you with a "great investment opportunity?"

In some cultures multiple generations live together in the same household, sharing chores such as child-care, cleaning, cooking, *and* sharing finances. Did you get that last part? It's an efficient way for everyone to pool resources and get the most bang for their buck. Families may be emotionally closer (than in our culture) due to the living arrangements. And I would bet that feuding is dealt with differently. It's harder to go "independent." In these same cultures, families often work and share business ventures together too.

But in mainstream America we definitely have the independent attitude. Our family structure and finances are strongly influenced by it. Our lives are a lot more separated, as are our wallets. So the real question here is, with families being as independent as they are in our culture, should finances be mixed in any way, as in investing money in something together?

Finances should be totally "mixed" for married couples without a doubt. But other than that it is NOT a good idea to "go in" with a family member (whether parents, kids, siblings, cousins, or in-laws) for investments of any kind, whether a business, land, home, vacation home, a timeshare, or to co-sign a loan of any kind.

But if you have money you don't mind watching swirl down the toilet, and truly won't have hard feelings against the family members who don't put in their fair share of money and elbow grease before crap hits the fan, then go ahead and invest away. Otherwise, consider these two big reasons not to invest money with family.

First, when a family member has a financial hardship and needs some cash (which is a given to happen eventually), they're probably going to want to get that cash from selling their share of the investment that you all went in on together. That may be you. The problem is, unless others are well off financially (which probably is *not* the case, otherwise you wouldn't have pooled your money together like stooges in the first place), they won't be able to buy you out. And that is when the resentments will start. Family get-togethers and Thanksgiving dinners will never be the same.

The second problem in this independent, lawsuit-happy culture is, well, you can guess the possible outcome scenarios involving flaky family members. You never think a family will go to court against each other, but it is more common than you might think. When people are broke and desperate and money is on the line, they can get ugly, even with family.

Please, don't take a boneheaded chance on ruining relationships with your family all because you went and bought some pathetic investment together that none of you could afford to buy in the first place. Instead, you can still all go on vacations together, stay in seedy motels, enjoy sub-standard cleaning and lumpy pillows and have a hell of a lot more fun without any guilt or blame games!

$$$$$$$

Chapter 30

It's All About Image

If you are a millionaire want-to-be or maybe some proud chested goon with a set of big silver balls hanging off the bumper of your Hummer, read this.

Trying to look rich before becoming rich is the surest way to stay in the poorhouse that I know of. This "wanting to look well-off" mentality has permeated moderate income earners, thanks to clever marketing and easy credit. Everyone wants to look more successful than they really are. There are so many ways we give in to wanting to look prosperous even though we're far from it. And it has gotten to the point where we will just not accept anything but the best and latest, from our cell phones to our palaces.

One of the most costly ways we "cave in" is in our chief purchase, our home. Instead of buying the size home we really need or can afford (or continuing to rent), we push the boundaries to the limit to commit to a huge house with extra rooms for our play things and even one just for the occasional guest. We want twice the square footage that our grandparents had, even though we have half the number of kids.

After all, we can't possibly ask our relatives to stay in a hotel when they visit. Or did it ever occur to us that it would be a lot cheaper to just pay for their hotel ourselves when they visit? Probably not. So instead, we sign up to be house-poor for the next thirty years and give our retirement money away as a free vacation hotel for our friends and family! Oh, this is a splendid plan because I'm sure they'll up the ante for us and overpay on their home as well. Then all of our vacation lodgings will be paid for life. Smart plan.

Do you think we're any smarter about our vehicles? After all, we have no problem with driving an older paid-for car, do we? Afraid we do. We love to appear affluent with our brand new his and hers rigs. We need "something dependable" and the manufacturers are offering great rebates, the banks even better rates. So let's continually sink a house payment worth of car payments into the garbage. Let's throw a couple of twenties out the window every single day just to look well-to-do! What an ingenious plan as well. I bet we'll get special treatment from the car dealer when we trade these in because, hey, they appreciate our immense purchasing power. More like they see our dunce caps from a mile away.

Do you mean to tell me that your cell phone can't access the internet? And you don't have a forty-two inch flat screen television yet? You poor soul. You still don't have that camper or RV? Oh please! And on and on we go with the ride to the crazy farm that never stops. We want to look so successful, ironically at the cost of ever actually getting there.

We must think there's no tomorrow, so just spend everything today. Well, if that *really* makes you happy, go for it. I don't see how it can. It certainly feels a lot better to not have the daily stress of worrying that if I lose my job I'll lose the whole lot because everything I "own" is tied up in a payment. What if I really didn't care so much about all the biggest, best, latest stuff?

But people must first choose between being rich or proud, because we really can't have both. I know this from the personal experience of getting completely out of debt by *temporarily* letting go of a lot of stuff,

actually everything. I can't tell you how good that felt.
Others have researched and written about this very topic
as well.

The best book I've read on the lifestyles of the rich
(and the pretenders) is called *The Millionaire Next Door*
by Thomas J. Stanley and William D. Danko. This book
was a real surprise to my way of thinking. They
interviewed millionaires and found a startling number of
them live in modest neighborhoods and drive boring
cars.

Many millionaires don't look rich! Many
millionaires got rich simply by living under their income
and saving the difference. And ironically they kept
doing this after it literally paid off. Once they became
rich they often no longer cared what people think, and
decided that not looking rich is much more satisfying
than showing off.

Today whenever I see people driving around in
fancy cars or living in huge houses, I immediately
assume they're not rich and I bet I'm right ninety nine
percent of the time.

So trade the "you're obviously not rich" image into
real wealth. And ditch the frickin' Hummer while
you're at it.

$$$$$$$

Chapter 31

If You're A Man

If you're a married man or a wanna be married man this is for you to consider, the next time you're feeling a little too macho for your own good, too big for your own pants. This is what real men do:

Real men go to a "her choice" lunch with their wives or girlfriends and order a Sandwich called "Queen" at a restaurant called "The Vegan."

Real men watch a biography on the Bee Gees with their wives, wake up with "Tragedy" running through their head, and don't bitch about the torture too much.

Real men go shopping with their wives and sit through the countless dressing room try-ons.

Real men babysit so their wives can go shopping.

Real men watch "chick flicks" with their wives and love it.

Real men wash dishes, pot and pans.

Real men know how to vacuum and mop.

Real men cook meals regularly with their wives.

Real men reserve lunch dates with their wife units.

Real men do a preliminary tax return estimate on Christmas night for one more surprise present for their wives.

Real men get out of debt for their wives.

Real men <u>work</u>, kill it and drag it home for their wives.

Real men plan out every month's spending with their wives, as in doing a big, bad Budget.

Real men spend most of their spare time with their family.

Real men would rather be with their wives than doing anything else.

$$$$$$$

Chapter 32

Good "In The Red"

Just how proud are you when it comes to the vehicle you drive? That kind of pride is costing many, many people their multi-millionaire status. Dick wads.

Several years ago, right after we married, my wife was driving home from work when she got rear-ended just a few blocks from home. The roads were extremely icy. Luckily she was not seriously injured. But her loyal friend "Red" was totaled, though it didn't necessary look like it should be. Because the roof and rear side panels were all one section, the cost of repairing the damage exceeded the book value for the then nine year old car.

Damn it! It was not a good time to lose Red. We didn't have the money to go buy another car and certainly weren't about to get a loan for one. Besides, she was paid for and in superb condition. My wife had bought it new and had taken excellent care of it. Red still looked like new inside and out and had relatively low miles as well, so there was lots of life left. We knew it would be difficult to go out and buy that much car for what we might get from the insurance.

But here's the kicker. The car was not damaged so terribly that our mechanic friend couldn't bang out the rear corner and replace the tale light assembly for about $400. The car had been valued at about $4900 and after we bought it back from the insurance company for $500 and paid our mechanical friend, we had a perfectly functional car and $4000 in our pocket. We just had to live with the big, crinkled, rusty pimple on the back of the car.

   We drove that car for another five years. First, it was part of our "get out of debt" plan, then our "pay off the house" plan. After that, at forty miles per gallon we just loved it. Good thing I have a wife who wasn't too proud to keep driving banged up ol' Red around. What a good reliable friend she turned out to be. The wife is pretty good too.

$$$$$$$

Chapter 33

Thrift Store Attitude

"I'm gonna pop some tags, only got twenty dollars in my pocket," so the song goes about thrift stores. Why would anyone want to rip off a thrift store anyway? Thrift stores rock.

So many stories from people who have actually gone from rags to riches can be summed up with this simple truth: They don't *have* to use thrift stores because they use thrift stores, or have the *thrift store attitude*.

But it's easy to think, "If I were rich, I'd do this and buy that and travel there..." But would you really?

Oh yes, if you suddenly won the lottery and or came into a surprise inheritance you probably *would* spend it like there's no tomorrow, ya nim rod. That is what usually happens with "easy come" money. It's becomes "easy go." The reason for this has to do with one's behavior with money. If your behavior with money has kept you broke, then even if a shit load of money is thrown in your face, you'll soon return to being a broke buffoon. A wise proverb says "A dog returns to its own vomit."

On the other hand, if you actually scrimped and saved and planned your way from rags to riches, then the money choices you made along the way will likely stick as part of your character and remain even after you get there. Why would you go through all the trouble to become wealthy, having learned the tricks to do it, only to blow it all away carelessly? You wouldn't, because the tricks become engrained. The actions become you.

What actions? Well for starters, things like this:

Checking for bargains at the thrift store, yard sales, want ads, and Craigslist even though you can afford to buy new.

Driving an older paid for car even though you can afford to buy any new car.

Taking more modest local vacations even though you can afford to fly to Hawaii or anywhere else. Better yet, throwing in some stay home vacations too.

Refusing to buy anything on credit, with the exception of your home (and only then if you have at least a twenty percent down payment and can pay it off in ten years).

When you go out to eat, going out for lunch instead of dinner.

Renting a home instead of buying until you're sure you can afford it easily on one income.

Renting stuff that you don't use frequently, like that pickup truck to haul an occasional load, or tools you only need once in a while.

Not collecting stuff. Instead, downsizing and selling off everything that is not used on a daily basis.

Saving as much money as you can, and investing it in diverse things.

Reading books on how to win with money.

Taking diligent care of your health by eating good foods because it will save you a bundle when you're older.

It's all about the thrift store attitude. It's so easy. Just don't pop any tags or you may find yourself doing hard time in more ways than one.

$$$$$$$

Chapter 34

Stay Vacations

Here's a great way to "cheap out" and be a tight ass on vacations, yet enjoy every frickin' moment.

Have you ever tried a stay at home vacation? I mean, not just a long weekend but a full week off from work just to stay at home? You should try it.

With a stay at home vacation you've eliminated the majority of your normal vacation expenses like travel and lodging. That's huge and it saves you a bundle.

Not only that, you effectively extend your vacation time since the days you would normally be traveling are now extra vacation days. Nice!

So now that you have all this time and money, what are you going to do!?

Get a massage. Try those restaurants you usually don't want to spend the money on. Take the kids to a sitter and go out on some dates. Go to the movie theatre several times. Rent a sports car for a few days! Do nothing. Sleep in. Order food to go or to be delivered. The possibilities are endless.

You have so much more control of *this* situation, so have the week of your life. You'll come back from *this* vacation a lot more rested, and a lot less poor!

$$$$$$$

Chapter 35

Travel With Your Parents

Here's another way to "cheap out" on vacations. There is definitely something cool to be said for traveling with your parents or parents-in-law, especially if you have kids.

You can save a lot of money by staying together. You can probably find a two or three bedroom place to rent by the week for less than it would cost each of you to stay separately in hotels. And chances are you'll actually have a lot more space for visiting and relaxing. Plus, with a kitchen you can save money on meals too.

Who knows, maybe your mother-in-law cooks amazing chicken and dumplings or your father is an expert with the barbeque! These more functional accommodations (as opposed to cramped motel rooms) will improve the quality of your vacation.

If it's possible to all travel in the same vehicle, then you'll not only have more time to visit during the trip, but spend much less on gas too. Let one person drive so everyone else can relax without the hassle. And there's another benefit of driving all together if you have kids.

We recently went on a road trip with my wife's parents and took their minivan. We sat in the front seats, her parents in the middle seats, and our four year old in the back seat. Guess who buffered all the "are we there yet" questions and questions? Not us! It was a nice break for a change.

Here's another side perk of driving together. If an elderly parent is handicapped, you have all the best parking spots everywhere you go!

Once you're at your favorite spot (ours is the Oregon coast), you have plenty of grandparent and grandchild bonding time. So there's more couple time with your spouse and that is always good. And of course, it's just plain fun to spend time together with your parents and make memories.

Oregon Coast, can't wait to see you again!

$$$$$$$

Chapter 36

A Myth You Ain't Rich

Okay, since you got this far in the book, maybe this won't apply to you. But surely you know some twit who still doesn't get it.

How do we learn and gain knowledge? While in some cultures story telling is how wisdom and experience are passed to the next generations, in most places throughout the world the most popular method is reading. Things are shifting though.

I wonder what percentage of ideas that reach our gray matter are cast into our homes, cars, and lives through television, radio, the internet, and our mobile devices. The majority of this information is for marketing purposes or else of brain fart quality.

Real learning comes from reading real books and serious writings. The bookstore and library (and some of the internet) are rich with it. Not sure who you can believe? Credibility is buried in the text of an author's writings and it makes itself known to the avid reader. *That* is why we must read and read, books, magazines, blogs, newspapers, online, offline, whatever.

We are losing touch in this area, friends. We are not reading, much less serious books or articles by writers doing it for the love of helping others. Hell, we're not even talking to each other anymore (emails and texting doesn't count). Instead we just want to be entertained.

Outlandishness is in fashion. Just look at the video counts on YouTube. Educational videos about personal finances and other self-help topics have only hundreds or thousands of views at most. Yet videos about ridiculous shit or some douche bag crashing himself into a wall? Tens of thousands, hundreds of thousands, or millions of views.

If we're getting all of our "higher education" from television, radio, and the trash-side-of-the-internet then we're letting the fox outfox us. That, actually, explains a lot considering it's reflected in the state of many people's financial affairs.

The fact is, if you want help on nearly any topic, if you want to wise up, wisdom is out there. And a lot of it is free these days. Get it while you can.

$$$$$$$

Chapter 37

Disco Madness

Let's move on to more serious subjects now, like Disco Dumb Shit Fever.

I love music. But there were times when the music of the day seemed to resemble my attitude toward saving. Both sucked.

Do you recall that jivy, bouncing dance music that seemed to displace the classic rock you loved? If you're old enough to remember a lot of the good rock bands bowing to the disco gods, then you'll also remember becoming more and more disenchanted with rock music about that time. It started to blow chunks and took decades to recover.

Can't say I ever loved disco music, in all its goofy glory. After all, didn't it usher in "glam" rock and all the even funkier costumes, over-the-top makeup, and big hair? But it had some fun moments. Or maybe that was the mind altering substances.

Aside from those "great" memories, it's too bad my savings and retirement planning didn't survive the polyester shirts and tight pants. Maybe you too forgot your retirement planning with the busted disco ball in the basement closet. Either way, back when we were hearing "Shake Your Booty" we should have been singing "Save Our Looty."

But if you're anything like me, those days are a bit of a blur and your retirement account is asking for a couple of aspirin.

Not to worry. It's never too late to shake it up! And I mean get extreme if you remember disco music and you're still behind the disco ball in your savings. If you need a whole gamut of ideas on how to get drastic, try my book *Money Prick: The Harsh Truth Your Friends Don't Have The Balls or Brains To Tell You.*

So, let disco come back in style if it wants. This time, you'll be able to afford some frilly fake polyester (real silk) shirts and look just as idiotic as back then, but in style.

$$$$$$$

Chapter 38

Rock and Roll Dream

Here's where the tires meet the pavement: your dreams. What are they? Do you have to wait until retirement to see them come true? Shit no! Be a rock star now!

How many stories have you heard about people retiring then dying not long afterwards? As a result, sometimes people wonder why they should bother with all this money planning when there's no guarantee how long they'll be able to enjoy it after retirement anyway. Why not just spend it all now? Ahh, you'll squander your real dreams, that's why. This is a true story.

My wife and I clawed our way out of debt in two years after selling virtually everything we owned. With no debt (except a mortgage) we felt we could work any job we wanted. But neither of us wanted to quit our job, just cut down on hours so we'd have more time together, for family, and for other interests.

So we both contacted our employers and asked if we could work less hours. With no debt you can do this with the confidence that if you *really* want to work less hours then you'll move on if your employer won't accommodate. We were both pleasantly surprised to find out that we could indeed change our working relationship with our employers and work less hours. Sure, this cost us money in smaller paychecks but now we had more TIME.

In my case, some of this extra time translated into writing a few rock and roll guitar tunes (my lifelong love). After making demo recordings of them, my wife, who was somewhat impressed with what I'd accomplished one afternoon, encouraged me to write a whole album worth of songs and record them. Since we had no extra debt I now had both the time and money to make this happen. And I did.

We paid cash for me to fly to Oklahoma City to record an album. While I didn't become a rock and roll star or anything like that, some pretty good stuff came out of it. I created some music I'm proud to share with others, and that I'll enjoy playing and listening to for the rest of my life! That was such a fun experience. But it would have been impossible to do while still a total slave to my job and the banks.

So…retirement schmirement! You don't need to wait until then to enjoy the some of the benefits of getting smarter with you money. Just get out of debt. You'll be able to pursue your lifelong interests now with the time and money to make them a reality! Come on, do it! It feels great. What are your dreams?

$$$$$$$

Chapter 39

Capture Memories

When you go places, look for something unique to that area to see or do. And fork out the money to do it. Otherwise, what is really the point? Traveling somewhere just to relax is great, but you can accomplish much of that in a stay at home vacation. Yes, get some R & R but don't just stick around your fancy hotel or resort. Venture out and about and find something outside the common tourist activities.

It may be a little risky or out of your comfort zone. It may involve a taxi ride with someone who doesn't speak your language. It may mean braving the elements, hot, windy, wet, or frigid. But you'll treasure the experience and the memory. Take lots of pictures. And I'm serious about this: Write down notes of your experience. Otherwise, the recollections will fade.

Case in point: The Ice and Snow World in Harbin, China. I just happened to be there one January on a short business trip with some coworkers. We were so busy each day with commuting and working that there was hardly any time left to eat dinner each night. But we had heard about the Ice and Snow World, opening just the week prior. So a group of us went one night. But it wasn't as easy as merely buying tickets and walking in the gate.

It was -18 C outside and windy that night. It was too far to walk from the hotel, so we got a cab. There had been a language barrier between us and the cab driver, who spoke no English. Nor did the woman who got in the taxi with us at our hotel, supposedly to buy us tickets to the ice show. We trustingly each gave her 300 RMB (about 48 bucks) for tickets and watched her ditch us not once, but twice before she actually got us inside the grounds of the ice show and then we never saw her again. We were relieved to find our taxi still waiting for us an hour and a half later when we'd had enough of the frigid cold.

While we walked about the enormous grounds, we were awestruck by the sheer size, number, and variety of the ice sculptures, snow sculptures and full-scale buildings, modeled using the architecture from numerous regions, made entirely of ice blocks that were fused together like brick and mortar. Making it even more magnificent was the colored lighting within the ice of every part of every building. And this night there was a near full moon in the black sky to frame the scene. This was a world class event, something you might see once in a lifetime.

Glad I was lucky enough to be there when it was going on. And yes, I took lots of pictures, although my fingers got so cold I could hardly feel the camera. Those are the kind of experiences that are hard to buy.

The trip home was just as interesting. I got stuck in Beijing. At first, I was a very unhappy camper, downright pissed off big time.

After that great evening of seeing the Ice and Snow World, we left the next morning for the insanely long flight back to the U.S. We arrived at the Harbin China airport promptly at 10:30 am, two hours before the flight to Beijing. It was a cold, clear morning and although it had been sunny all week it seemed clearer and brighter that day. Maybe that was because we were going home. Beijing is where we would catch the international flight back to the United States.

Our trip had gone well. A coworker and I had visited a food plant in Harbin to assess existing equipment in preparation for an expansion. We had met an international project team with members from Canada, the United Kingdom, and China. We all had worked, commuted, and ate together for three days and walked around the city in the bitter cold evenings. The Ice and Snow World on the last night had been awesome. It was a productive and unforgettable time. A lot of activities had been crammed into several days in almost a blur and now it was time to leave.

At the airline ticket counter, I presented my passport and hoped there would be no problem getting my boarding passes all the way to San Francisco. I was caught off guard and a little concerned to only be given a boarding pass to Beijing just the minor few hour hop away, with instructions that I would have to get the boarding pass for the other major leg of the trip once I got to Beijing.

More disconcerting was the fact that my coworker got his boarding passes all the way through to San Francisco, though our tickets were supposedly the same. But they assured me that there was something different with my ticket so there was nothing more they could do. Wouldn't do me any good to make a scene in a strange land. I had an uneasy feeling because we were only to be in Beijing barely an hour and a half.

The fact that we were late leaving Harbin by about a half an hour didn't help my apprehension. And by the time we landed at Beijing and taxied forever, got off the plane at what seemed like the furthest gate out and hustled the long way to the nearest ticket counter, another fifteen minutes had burned up. But I was thinking "we have at least a half hour to board the plane so, no problem." Wrong! I was told that boarding passes could not be issued within one hour of the flight. I was out of luck. Remember my coworker who had his boarding pass? I wished him luck as he ran on to his gate. Yep, he made it, just barely.

If I was lucky, maybe the next flight for me would be later in the day. So I made my way upstairs to the main international ticket counter. But they only confirmed my sneaking suspicion that the next flight would be the next day at the same time. They would arrange for a bus to take me to a hotel, and warned that I would be sharing a room unless I wanted to pay extra. Great!

More than a few choice words were muttered as I stepped away from the counter. Oh, I was feeling so pissed off I could hardly think straight. This is why I hated traveling for work, giving up my fucking weekend, fucking around in this fucking airport, wasting a bunch of fucking time.

And as the sinking feeling began to hit me that, yes, I was really stuck here another twenty-four hours without knowing a soul or speaking the language, I heard it: Music, but not music to uplift my soul. No, as if to enhance the sinking feeling of defeat, Beethoven's Moonlight Sonata was steadily streaming through the airport on the loud speakers! Oh, what perfect music to set the mood! Though I was aware of the irony, I felt even more irritated at the turn of events in just the last fifteen minutes.

So, as I stood there fuming and waiting for the bus, I imagined what a hassle this was going to be. Being stuck in Beijing was a little more nerve-racking than just being ditched at the ice show. I imagined all sorts of potential issues like not getting back to the airport in time the next day due to some miscommunication and missing my flight again. As much as I would have enjoyed some sightseeing around Beijing, I didn't want to take the chance. In fact, I was skeptical about leaving the airport at all.

Maybe it would be better to just stay in the airport all night. I'd done that before. As I pondered the options, out of the corner of my eye I noticed a colorfully dressed young woman walking towards me, cheerfully pushing a cart loaded with big flowery suitcases. She looked at home here, Chinese I assumed, so I was a little surprised when she said to me in perfect English, "The bus is coming now."

Turns out that Ying, a Chinese college student finishing school in Canada, had missed her flight to New York. However, unlike me who had my flight lined up for the next day, she was put on a waiting list so wasn't even sure to get out the next day. But she didn't seem upset at all and explained that she always figures to get delayed coming or going on every trip. Hmm, guess I needed to take a chill pill.

The bus was new, the commute short, and the hotel seemed nice enough too. They supplied a free dinner so after leaving my stuff in my room I went to the restaurant and sat down. It was not your typical sit down and order from the menu type of place. You sit down at these large round tables and they bring you what they bring you. There were only a few other people sitting around, not looking happy. One older Norwegian gentleman at my table complained that the service in China had been declining for thirty years. Ying came in and joined our table.

When the food came, I thought it looked like it must be a traditional Chinese meal of Beijing cabbage, beef and vegetables, bean sprouts and egg, rice, and egg flower soup. Ying was surprised that I could use chopsticks. I told her that my wife and I loved Chinese food. This food seemed pretty good to me. Curious of what Ying thought, I asked her how she would rate this meal on a scale of 1 to 10 (10 is best). She said 3. American Chinese restaurants must be doing us a disservice.

The older gentleman looked disapprovingly at the food and said he didn't want beef. So Ying spoke to the servers in Chinese, asking if the Norwegian could have chicken instead. They served him a spicy chicken version and he later said the meal was very good and looked like his mood had greatly improved.

A few Beijing beers later and a lot of questions to Ying, I had learned quite a bit more about China, how they all learn English in school from a young age, the long hours they generally work, the high cost of housing, and several Chinese words. Ying also told me about her parents, her boyfriend, college, and her favorite foods. I told her about my wife and kids, and adventures on this trip to China.

Meeting Ying was really enjoyable and my attitude about being stuck in Beijing had sure changed. And before I knew it, it was time to call it a night. One of the last things Ying said to me before I left the restaurant was "Okay, I don't know you but I think you talk too much today." I laughed and told her it was probably the beer talking or, using one of my new Chinese words, "juping."

What a great experience. But get this, if I wouldn't have taken the time on the flight home to actually write down everything I could remember about the trip on a note pad, it would be only a blur now and I could never have recounted this story.

Oh, and when you travel, don't forget a bottle of high strength chill pills.

$$$$$$$

Chapter 40

Balancing Act

Do you want to become the ultimate success in your field of interest (including if it's just to become rich)? If you think you would, then go for it! But be careful that it doesn't come at an even greater price, like your sorry OCD ass.

You will find a common theme in the biographies of highly successful people. Whether they are thriving business owners, musicians, or actors you will find an unusual degree of focus and dedication to the craft. Perhaps even an obsession. There is no need to get into the psychological reasons for this immense passion, but the Obsessive Compulsive Disorder likely includes a strong sense of having to prove oneself.

There is something else that these "stars" have in common too. They work their asses off. Being the best will require long, late hours of continual study, practice and more practice. Because of the extreme time commitment, many (not all) of these icons are unable to maintain healthy relationships in their personal lives.

At some point a decision is made, whether conscious or unconscious, to continue pursuing the one real love. As a result, marriages and other relationships with family can suffer for it. Dumb Shits! Of course, maybe I'm just jealous because I never reached my lifelong dream of being a rock star lead guitarist icon.

It is not physically possible to be the best at everything, as there simply is not enough time. Therefore, to excel unusually high in one area will cost you in another, plain and simple. If you want to develop your own thriving business it will cost you. If you want to become the best rock guitarist ever it will cost you. If you want to make it on the silver screen it will cost you.

The momentous feats will cost you time, money, sweat and tears, and maybe many relationships along the way. Shoot for the stars, yes. But make sure the target is worth the sacrifice. It may be better to settle for that local yokel musician award.

While you're heading for stardom, strive for a balance between *your* thing and the *other* important things in life. Otherwise, that OCD may take total control, turning you into a paranoid, reclusive germ-a-phobe, unable to enjoy the money machine you created.

$$$$$$$

Chapter 41

On The Edge

When I was a teenager living in Montana, my
friends and I used go to many keg o' beer parties out by
the river or up in the mountains, the further from town
the better. Given some of the stupid things we did, it's a
wonder we're still here to tell about them.

At one such party by the river, we were laughing
and standing around the fire pit as usual, smoking
cigarettes, passing around an occasional joint and just
having a grand old time. Suddenly, on the road just
above us, a car slowly rolled along, then we sawing
flashing lights. Now this is always your worst
nightmare at these bashes, being busted by the cops.
Usually ninety eight percent of us were underage
drinkers.

At first we all started freaking out. "Cops,"
someone yelled and then mayhem. Stuff got thrown into
the fire, people ran into the bushes, some ran to their
cars, and splashes of beer bottles could be heard in the
river.

Then, something surprising happened. The flashing
lights stopped and the car raced on by. A quick glance
at the car as the fire light reflected off the driver's side
revealed that it was none other than a familiar early
seventies Mercury Cougar driven by a punk we used to
call, Narc.

There was only one thing to do, chase the punk
down and teach him a lesson. I quickly volunteered to
drive my '72 Toyota Celica to try and catch the little

bastard. So three of my friends piled in the car with me and we pealed out of there after the Cougar.

I don't know what I was thinking, assuming I could out run a Cougar. But I did know this: I was two steps crazier and probably more experienced at driving, so we'd give it a go anyway.

He stayed hundreds of yards or more ahead of us, but never quit got out of our sights. We followed him the nearly twelve miles towards town and then he turned off on a back road and cut over to the old two lane highway that went to Butte, twenty three miles to the West.

I knew this road well, having driving to Butte many a time that way. The road crossed through the mountains about half way to Butte, and there were many switchbacks and S-curves to navigate. If we lost him on the curves, he could turn off somewhere ahead of us without notice. We had to catch him.

Adrenaline pumped as we pushed at speeds up to a hundred miles an hour on the straightaways. We began to catch up and stayed on his ass all the way into the mountains. "We're going to catch him on the curves," I shouted, because I knew he would never drive as crazy fast as me on those curves. He was close in our sights as we approached the mountain curves and we were gaining on him.

On some of the straightaways he gained more distance. On the curves we'd make it up. He was just a hundred yards ahead. But we were almost to the hair pin curve section on the descent from the top of the mountain pass. I was still certain we'd catch him on the sharp curves.

As we hit the slopping curves heading down the mountain, we'd seeing him after rounding a curve, they he'd disappear around the next one. Then we'd see him after we rounded that one and he'd disappear again around the next. The bald tires on my Celica squealed loudly around every curve, just like in the movies. We were all hooting and hollering.

After getting around the last of the worst of the curves, we couldn't see the Cougar anymore. "What the fuck?" someone said from the back seat. "Where is he?"

We pressed on even faster, but never saw another glimpse of him. "Maybe he crashed over the edge," someone else said.

The reply from the passenger seat was, "Good, fucking narc."

We eventually admitted defeat, turned around and headed back to Whitehall. But we laughed all the way back about the chase and how we squealed the tires around all those corners like a stunt car chase in a bad ass movie.

It's a wonder we're not dead. It's a wonder *I'm* not dead because I routinely did driving stunts like this.

Looking back, I can see that this same bull in the china shop, pedal to the metal, both guns blazing, chuck the rock before thinking attitude is what got me into trouble with money, over and over. I was totally "live for the moment" and it showed in my having no money after three decades of working. What a jerk.

$$$$$$$

Chapter 42

Tuesday's Gone

Several years ago I watched a re-run of *My Name Is Earl* and heard a familiar song: *Tuesday's Gone* by Lynyrd Skynyrd. Funny how a few lines of a song can take you back to another time. Suddenly, I was reminded of my teenage years and my good friends back then. Lynyrd Skynyrd was one of our favorite groups. We loved music and partying. We had a rock band named High Voltage.

High Voltage was Screaming Dean on keyboards and vocals, Mellow Merle on bass, Mountain Bob on drums, and Mad Me on guitar and vocals. We were often joined by Mustang Jim on guitar and Crazy Kim on a very entertaining guitar and vocals with his "on the fly" wild adlib songs. We can't forget comical Brian "Barney," either. Those were fun times, hanging out, partying, driving crazy, playing loud music and dreaming of being rock stars.

Not long after those rock and roll days I moved away from that small town, put my rock star dreams on hold, went to college, and eventually moved a few states away for work. And the years turned into decades. I lost touch with the friends of my youth. Over the years there have been many times that I wondered what became of them or where they were. But I never really tried to find out. Life just got too busy with work and family and all.

Nowadays it's pretty easy to hop online and figure out where someone is. Recently I located a few of my old music buddies and contacted them. It was really cool to hear Bob's voice on the phone after all these years. He surprisingly sounded the same! It was great to email Dean and see some pictures of him on the internet. He surprisingly looked the same too, though grayer.

But when I thought about the song *Tuesday's Gone*, I felt a sadness. Not only is Tuesday gone, but so is Wednesday, Thursday, and half of Friday. Life is short. Many of the people who pass into your life, pass out of it before you've had a chance to really make any lasting impression, aside from a negative immature one. Or you move on too soon to experience their full impact on your life.

What can you do?

$$$$$$$

Chapter 43

Too Old to be Young & Too Young to be Old

For all you male mid-life crisis cases, listen up. Don't buy the sports car convertible to show off your balding comb-over head. Don't go after the blond bimbo, big boob, no brain wonder who is twenty years younger than you. Don't buy a gym membership thinking the new sexier you is going to make a shit of difference to anyone. There's something better than all that.

I know it hurts to be getting older. It really sucks when younger people view you as old, and the gray hairs see you as a young whipper snapper. Where has life flown?

Perhaps you're from the "baby boomer" generation. Having worked for longer than you have left to work, you're starting to count down the years to when you don't have to go into work anymore. It's still a long ways off but you find yourself thinking of it more and more.

If you're an older chap, you've probably cut back on some of your frivolous spending too, after looking at your weak investment statements. You started saving too late, spent too much over the years, and now have too much time to make up for.

To make things worse, you're in the midst of another mid-life crisis. You went ahead and bought the bloody sports car. And you tried some partying like in your youth only to find you're now a big, sorry wimp. Your round balding head is protruding ever more, as is your belly.

So what's left?

Whether you see it or not, you're actually in your prime. You're probably still pretty healthy. You're probably making more money than ever in your life. Your kids are probably grown or mostly so. You're in a good spot!

Don't get caught up in things! Get caught up in the moments. Smell the coffee. Spend time with people you love. Do some good. Sure, save away all the money you can and forget about it. But make life more about enjoying things that don't cost money.

As much as you might wish you could go back in time to fix all your stupidity with money, it's too late. You've already blown a wad like your dog heaving up your kid's pet hamster. Get over it. You're not going to get another chance like this, right now. Make what's left count.

$$\$\$\$\$\$\$\$$

Chapter 44

Money, Money, Money

Don't misunderstand my last key point about dough: There is nothing fundamentally wrong with making money or having money, even lots of it. But there *is* a hazard associated with money that is worth paying attention too, in case we fall into a dangerous trap.

When the behavior that kept us broke and in debt is suddenly and radically changed like a wildfire, to an intense desire to never be foolish with money again, or to go the extra mile to become wealthy, we run the risk of going too far the other way if we're not prepared. Thinking we're just being frugal, we can suddenly transition from careless to cheapskate. We can morph like molding cheese from an open handed giver to a stingy closed fisted, tight assed, diamond producer.

You probably know people who seem to care only about money. Money, money, money. We all have to on guard. My wife and I, too, are frequently focused on it. We often discuss money together, perhaps every day in some way. We write about it. And in our relationships with friends and family it seems that the subject of money always comes up, and we always have a strong opinion about it. Have we gone too far the other way?

Planning and discussing your finances is wise. Money is a great tool for buying time and resources to pursue our dreams. Money allows us to help others and make a difference while we're alive (and maybe even after we're gone!).

It is the *love* of money that causes the problems. If getting more and more money is the main goal, then when it's time to pull out the bottle of champagne to toast your so called success, your head is going to be so far up your ass that sipping from a wine glass will be the least of your problems.

If we make our lives all about getting more and more money, then we have missed the point of even having it. If it's always all about the money, then at the end of our lives we will have gained nothing and done nothing of real significance. And we won't be taking it with us either. In fact, after you're gone some other cheap, lazy bastards who haven't worked for it and never even liked you will spend all your hard earned money like there's no tomorrow, buying the kind of shit to make you roll over in your cardboard box.

This money-thing is a real balancing act. On one athlete's foot, if you don't have it you must work far too much to just get by. On the other fungus infested appendage, if you're great at making lots of money then you may also be spending way too much time working. Both of these options leave us little time for a balance that's truly rich.

So each of us must answer this question: When is enough, enough? Is it as long as I have the basics of food, shelter and clothing? Is it when I'm out of debt? Is it when I own my house? Is it when my net worth is a million dollars?

Once I'm doing better financially, at what point will I back off a little, or a lot, and enjoy life along the way too?

$$$$$$$

That's All Folks!

Two Last Things For Your Consideration

Thing #1: Your Input Matters

Thank you so much for reading my book. If you enjoyed it, would you be so kind as to leave a review at your favorite online book retailer? Your review may help other curious readers to check out my book! And I'd really appreciate your feedback on all my hard work. Thanks again for your time.

Thing #2: Other Books You Might Enjoy

If you enjoyed this book, chances are you'll enjoy some of these other books as well, currently available as ebooks that are downloadable in just about every format at Smashwords.com, Amazon.com, and your other favorite online retailers. You'll also find the links to all seven of these books at boileddownmoneygoo.com.

Breaching The Guardian Dimension, by Cory Richardson.
Topic: Spokane, Washington area in eighty years. Two girls' relationship, crime, revenge.
Description: Coming of age in the 2090's, friends Marcus, Randi, Vamir and Meagan find themselves working at a prestigious government-funded supernatural research facility. Something goes wrong after Marcus' very first "exposure." His friends watch in disbelief as other employees mysteriously die right after their first exposures. It is not clear whether they're

victims of machine malfunctions, the guardians or something else. During the mayhem, Randi and Meagan find the "something more" in their relationship that Randi has been longing for all along. Like their favorite song, it's para, para, paradise. But something connected to the research program dooms the girls' alliance. WARNING: Contains some adult themes (lesbian encounters), but nothing graphic.

Silicon Facades, by Cory Richardson.

Topic: Our digital future, depraved society, and twisted justice.

Description: How our online presence in the early 2000's evolved into the government's digital social tool of the 2130's to pigeonhole citizens into social classes and control their every activity, even where babies come from. In 2133, Darren and his pregnant wife, Amber, a smart, drop dead stunning, blue-eyed brunette, desperately seek ingenious and mostly criminal methods to raise their status, having dropped to the lowest social class because of circumstances affecting their government issued Score. Take the roller coaster ride with the exploits of Darren and Amber and their shocking nonconformist ways of playing against the system's outrageous rules.

Money Prick, The Harsh Truth Your Friends Don't Have The Balls Or Brains To Tell You, by Taylor Young.

Topic: Personal finances with a crass humor spin.

Description: You're in luck. You just found the most enjoyable, hilarious book you'll ever read on a typically not-so-fun topic; family/personal finances. Even if you know all this stuff already, it's worth reading just for the laughs! WARNING: If you are offended by some crass language, then maybe this book isn't for you.

How I Lost A Million Dollars Twice, And Other Brilliant Adventures, by Taylor Young.

Topic: Personal finance tales you'll shake your head over.

Description: Through a bizarre twist of circumstances, follow Taylor's eclectic accounts of kissing goodbye a couple million dollars by a ripe ol' young age. Enjoy someone else's misery while you learn what not to do with your time and money thanks to Young's numb skull, painful lessons. Maybe some of these things can save your butt from a good kicking. WARNING: If you are offended by some crass language, then maybe this book isn't for you.

No Good Deed Goes Unpunished, by Taylor Young.

Topic: A collection of laugh out loud humorous and outrageous deeds, based on true stories.

Description: From time to time it's entertaining to watch others squirm in hot water. The mean streak in us loves stories of woe – especially when it involves someone else. Sometimes, we are the blundering idiots with a tale of despair for others to be pleased about. Either way, the good deeds that don't go unpunished make such juicy stories!

Why You Can't See God, by David Lavy.

Topic: Is there real evidence for God's existence?

Description: One of the most provocative and to-the-point dialogues broached on this topic in years. No one can have a neutral reaction to this book; you'll either applaud its audacity or be disgusted by it, crass language and all. You may wonder whether fans of Mr. Lavy's book are in short supply, judging by some of the online jabs. What is all the fuss about, anyway? Is it really as bad as they say, or has a big ol' nerve been struck?

Boiled Down Money Goo, Tips For Propelling Your Financial Future, by Daniel and Deborah Minteer.

Topic: Lighthearted, fun, and to-the-point summaries of personal finance topics (the "cleaned up" version of Money Prick).

Description: Boiled Down Money Goo is a painless way to learn about a sometimes painful subject - personal finances. With a dose of humor to help it sink in, these simple, boiled down personal finance tips will outfit you in the best possible gear to weather the financial mudslides. While grandma may give similar advice, we won't dump it on your plate along with a lumpy bran and prune muffin...or flash any dentures.

****

About Taylor Young

Seattle, Washington native Taylor Young is a musician, engineer, book author, and family man.

"I love writing, whether song lyrics, technical papers, ranting in a blog, or more thought out topics worthy of a book. It's remarkable that writers today have a voice through online publishing. So much more time is freed up for letting the creative juices flow, which instead used to be spent pursuing and persuading publishers. The world benefits from this new freedom and I'm glad to be a part of it."

Contact Taylor at tyoung395@hotmail.com

www.ingramcontent.com/pod-product-compliance
Lightning Source LLC
Chambersburg PA
CBHW051708170526
45167CB00002B/581